Dowd's History of
LIMERICK

A PERSPECTIVE VIEW of the
CITY of LIMERICK
taken from Alderman Crips's House
on the North Strand

Sponsored by

LIMERICK TREATY 300

DOWD'S
History of
LIMERICK

by

Rev James Dowd BA TCD

New Edition

Editor

Cian O'Carroll

Consultant Historian Liam Irwin

ILLUSTRATED

THE O'BRIEN PRESS
DUBLIN 1990

THIS EDITION FIRST PUBLISHED 1990 BY THE O'BRIEN PRESS LTD.20 VICTORIA ROAD, DUBLIN 6, IRELAND IN ASSOCIATION WITH LIMERICK TREATY 300. ORIGINAL PUBLISHED IN 1890 BY G. McKERN & SONS, PUBLISHERS OF LIMERICK.

10 9 8 7 6 5 4 3 2 1

British Library Cataloguing in Publication Data
Dowd, James
Dowd's History of Limerick.-2nd.ed.
1.Limerick (County). Limerick, history
I. Title II. O'Carroll, Cian
941.945
ISBN 0-86278-221-X

Typesetting: The O'Brien Press
Cover Separations: The City Office Dublin
Book Design: Michael O'Brien
Printing: SciPrint, Shannon
Cover Picture: 19th century painting,
The Siege of Limerick, by K. MacManus

MTG

The publishers wish to thank the following
for their kind permission to reproduce illustrations:

Mrs Dorothy Colthurst page 11
Limerick City Library pages 48 and 49
Joseph MacMahon page 97, 115
The National Library title page
and pages 32, 70, 78, 83, 105, 108, 123
Cian O'Carroll: back cover
Celie Rahilly (Limerick Corporation)
and John Buckley: map.

Contents

Introduction

THIS BOOK WAS FIRST PUBLISHED IN MARCH 1890 by McKerns of Limerick but has been out of print for many years. The author, James Dowd, at that time correctly described it as a sketch rather than a scholarly work. It is quite different in treatment and style from the better known histories of Limerick, written by people such as Ferrar, Fitz Gerald and McGregor or indeed Lenihan. However, as a popular and very readable history of the city, covering the period from earliest times up to the end of the 19th century, it is an absorbing piece of work. Re-publication is now particularly appropriate in order to mark the celebration of 'Limerick Treaty 300'.

Rev James Dowd, a Church of Ireland curate, like many of his clerical contemporaries took considerable interest in local history and antiquities. He was born in 1848 and some years after his death in 1909 a memorial window to him was erected in St. Mary's Cathedral, Limerick. It depicts him appropriately, dressed both as a young clergyman and in old age. The window, probably designed by Michael Healy and made at the Tower of Glass Studios in Dublin, is a fine example of early 19th-century Irish stained glass. Rich colour and celtic ornament is featured in the two window panels.

No information has yet come to hand in regard to James Dowd's exact place of birth, or early education. It is likely that he was born in Limerick city. However, he had a distinguished career in Trinity College, Dublin, which he entered in 1870. There he obtained a Mathematical and First Science Scholarship in 1873.

In 1874, he took his B.A. degree and was awarded a gold medal in science. He obtained the Divinity Testimonium in the same year, and was also ordained in that year by the Bishop of Cashel, for the County Tipperary — later transferring to the Limerick diocese. He spent most of his life as a Diocesan Curate in Limerick city and county and filled numerous Diocesan offices, amongst them the very important one of

Diocesan Secretary, to which he was appointed in 1887.

Rev James Dowd was an eminent mathematical and classical scholar, and his name had for many years been prominently identified with religious education and historical research. He was a most popular preacher, with a relaxed and convivial personality. He devoted a considerable amount of his time to municipal affairs, notably to the Limerick Free Library. His fellow committee members included James Frost, J.P., and Very Rev Father Lee, P.P.

James Dowd's wife was a Miss Hosford whose family owned the *Limerick Chronicle*. Dowd's daughter, Mossie, married a Rev Colthurst, Rector of Clarina. Dowd's sister-in-law, Jane Hosford, was a governess and married Fred Cleeve of Fernbank (now Salesian Convent). His son Reginald, born in 1883, subsequently had a successful career in the British Foreign Service.

At the time of the author's death in 1909, he lived at 7 Swanson Terrace, O'Connell Avenue. He was buried at Clarina, Co. Limerick.

His published work includes this present volume as well as *Round About the County of Limerick*, published in 1896, *History of St. Mary's Cathedral*, published in 1899, 'Old Limerick', articles in *Journal of Limerick Field Club*, published in 1897-1900.

The editor and publishers wish to thank the following for their kind assistance in preparing this book for re-publication: Liam Irwin and other members of the Educational and Cultural Committee, Limerick Treaty 300; Tom Morris, MacKerns; Dr Robert Cussen; Very Rev Dean Talbot; Mary Nagle; Marlene O'Connor, F.A.S.; Joseph MacMahon; Celie Rahilly; John Buckley; *Limerick Leader*; National Library, Dublin; and the following relatives of Rev James Dowd: Rev W.R. Colthurst, Armagh; Mrs Dorothy Colthurst, Cork.

Some minor revisions have been made to the text in the interests of clarity and ease of understanding. The illustrations, however, are completely new as the quality of the originals was relatively poor.

CIAN O'CARROLL
June, 1990

Preface to the 1890 Edition

Rev James Dowd, c. 1895

THIS SKETCH OF LIMERICK AND ITS SIEGES, as well as other notes concerning the places of chief historic interest in the County of Limerick, were put together by the writer more for his own information than with any eye towards their publication, at least in a book form. Whatever time could be spared from other occupations was employed some years ago in collecting and throwing into readable form whatever could be got together respecting the castles and abbeys, so many of which are to be found dotted over the County of Limerick, and concerning which so little is popularly known. In the pursuit of such a study the City of Limerick must of course have occupied the most important place, for to omit it would be like leaving out the part of Hamlet in the play. The whole was to some extent completed and the manuscript had been laid aside for the last five or six years, though portions have occasionally found their way into print. When the present publishers learned a few months ago of the existence of such a manuscript, they immediately entered into arrangements for the publication of that part relating to the City of Limerick. It is owing to their enterprise that the following pages are given to the public. This is not the first time that the firm of G. McKern and Sons has been connected with a History of Limerick, for Fitz Gerald's and McGregor's work, published in 1827, bears their name upon the title page. It is now my pleasing duty to acknowledge the obligations I am under to my predecessors in this field of research, to Ferrar, Fitz Gerald and McGregor, already referred to, and especially to Mr Maurice Lenihan, whose *History of Limerick* will ever remain a monument of that writer's industry and research and a record invaluable to all subsequent explorers. I have also to acknowledge the valuable assistance I have received from Mr James Frost, J.P., whose minute and at the same time extensive knowledge of everything relating to Irish antiquities and Irish history is rarely surpassed. Mr Frost not only afforded me ready access at all times to his valuable collection of works of reference, but most kindly pointed out sources of information with which I was not previously acquainted, and finally was good enough to look over some of the sheets as they were going through the press. To Mr J. G. Barry, J.P., the work is indebted for the notes on pages 116 and 122. It was by no means easy to secure such an illustration of St. John's Cathedral as would do justice to the spire and building, but the difficulty was removed by the architect, Mr Hennessy, who supplied a photograph, from which the plate for the illustration facing page 144 [not included in this edition] has been prepared. The Coloony Medal, which is extremely rare, was placed at the service of the publishers by Mr George Hewson, M.A., of Hollywood, Adare. I have now only to express the hope that the perusal of *Limerick and its Sieges* may be found as interesting by the public as its preparation was by the author.

JAMES DOWD
March, 1890

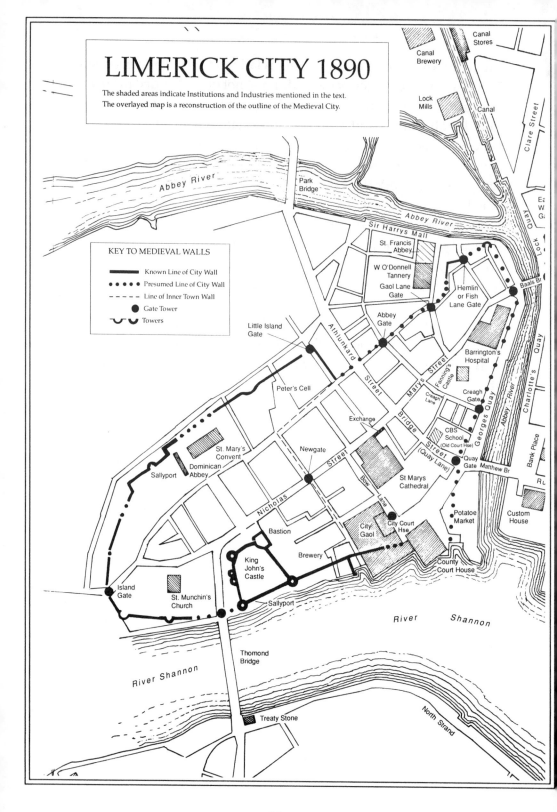

LIMERICK CITY 1890

The shaded areas indicate Institutions and Industries mentioned in the text.
The overlayed map is a reconstruction of the outline of the Medieval City.

KEY TO MEDIEVAL WALLS

— Known Line of City Wall
•••• Presumed Line of City Wall
- - - Line of Inner Town Wall
● Gate Tower
Towers

Abbey River

Canal Stores
Canal Brewery
Lock Mills
Canal
Clare Street

Park Bridge

Abbey River

Sir Harrys Mall

St. Francis Abbey
W O'Donnell Tannery
Gaol Lane Gate
Hemlin or Fish Lane Gate
Baals Br

Little Island Gate

Athlunkard Street

Abbey Gate

Barrington's Hospital

Peter's Cell

Mary's Street

Fanning's Castle

Creagh Lane

Creagh Gate

Georges Quay

Abbey River

Charlotte's Quay

Exchange

Bridge Street (Quay Lane)

CBS School (Old Court Hse)

Quay Gate

Matthew Br

Bank Place

St. Mary's Convent

Dominican Abbey

Newgate

Nicholas Street

St Marys Cathedral

Sallyport

Bow Lane

Custom House

Bastion

Brewery

City Gaol

City Court Hse

Potatoe Market

King John's Castle

County Court House

Island Gate

St. Munchin's Church

Sallyport

River Shannon

Thomond Bridge

River Shannon

North Strand

Treaty Stone

Ea W Ga

Quay

Lock

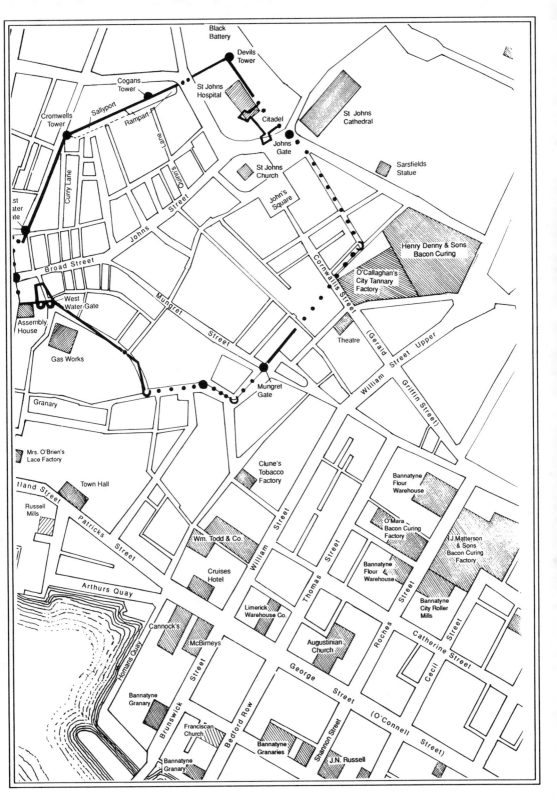

CHAPTER I

Limerick Under
The Danes

THE ORIGIN OF THE CITY OF LIMERICK is hidden in obscurity. The ancient form 'Luimneach', occurs in our annals long before the city itself could have existed. It seems to have been applied first to the estuary of the Shannon,[1] and at some subsequent period became the designation of the city on its banks. The earliest mention of Luimneach occurs in connection with a partition of the Island at such a remote period as the 12th century before the Christian era; and a similar reference occurs when another partition took place eleven hundred years later.

The references to Luimneach prior to the arrival of the Danes are neither numerous nor important. One of the innumerable battles of the 3rd century took place there in 241. In 378 Crimhthan, Monarch of all Ireland, died whilst approaching the neighbourhood, under the following circumstances: the issue of Eochy, King of Ireland, being too young to succeed him, his brother-in-law, Crimhthan, was raised to the throne, which he occupied for thirteen years, and during this period he carried his arms into Scotland and even as far as Brittany. In the meantime his nephews arrived at man's estate. Their mother, sister to Crimhthan, resolved to place her son Brian on the throne at all hazards, even at the expense of her own life. She prepared a poisoned draught for her brother, and of which she previously partook in his presence. Crimhthan then journeying southward was attacked with the pangs of death on the summit of the Cratloe Hills, and there he expired and was buried.[2] The object sought for by such criminal means was not accomplished, and the monarchy passed

17

away from the Munster dynasty to a northern Chieftain. The states elected Niall of the Nine Hostages to the vacant throne, in whose family the succession continued for six centuries, till Brian Boru again secured the sovereignty for the southern states.

In the middle of the 5th century the neighbourhood was visited by St. Patrick, who gained many converts to Christianity, amongst whom was Carthen, the Chief of a district adjacent to Killaloe, who was baptised, with many of his followers at Saingeal, now Singland. St. Patrick remained some time in this part of the country, and ordained St. Nessan, founder of Mungret. He may have also consecrated St. Manchin; but there is not the slightest authority for calling him Bishop of Limerick.[3] It is quite certain that the Church of Donoughmore, about two miles south of the city, was founded by St. Patrick. At Singland his well and 'bed' are pointed out to the present day. St. Patrick did not cross into Thomond at this time, but proceeded to Finnine, a place that has not been fully identified, but is probably Knockpatrick. Here he gave his blessing to the people of North Munster who had received him so kindly, and foretold concerning 'the Green Island in the West' (Scattery Island) near the mouth of the river, that 'the lamp of the people of God should shine in it', a prophecy fulfilled in the person of St. Senan.

The authentic and continuous history of Limerick may be said to commence with the arrival of the Danes on our western shores. These hardy rovers from the shores of the Baltic and the German Ocean appeared first in Ireland in the year 795. They paid only flying visits for the purpose of plunder, and it was not till 831 that their war ships appeared in the Luimneach, as it was then called, and advancing as far as they could inland, anchored at length at the extremity of what is now known as the King's Island, and set about plundering the adjacent country. The advantages of the site – the wealth and fertility of the neighbouring country – the facility of access in their light sailing galleys – and the ready means of penetrating into the interior of the Island – all these were attractions which were not overlooked. They returned shortly afterwards in large numbers. The intruders fortified themselves in their new acquisition. Limerick came into existence as

A view of the River Shannon from St. Mary's Cathedral.

a Danish colony, and the centre from which radiated their expeditions.

The ravages of these ruthless invaders extended in all directions – for the whole country lay at their mercy. They spared neither age nor sex, and their track was marked with desolation. The condition of the people was truly pitiable, for to the evils arising from the senseless dissensions of the native Chieftains were now added the attacks of an enemy, brave, cruel, and pitiless. The Danes directed their energies to the extinction of religion and learning. The schools and colleges which had made Ireland the luminary of the West were destroyed, and the students slain or scattered. The monasteries and other homes of piety were burned to the ground, or handed to pagan priests to celebrate the mysteries of Odin and Thor. The clergy were murdered at their altars – the monks in their cells. Almost every manuscript and record of the past perished in the flames. Their daring was unbounded. In 843 the Danes actually penetrated to Armagh, carried off the Primate, his relics and his people, to their fleet at 'Luimneach'.

The Danes could not have held their ground for a day were the Irish united amongst themselves. Not seldom do we find the Irish in alliance with the Danes against their own countrymen. Occasionally the invaders suffered severe losses. The O'Donovans slaughtered many of them in 834; and fifty years later the men of Connaught revenged their frequent inroads. Cormac MacCuilennan, King of Cashel, in his brief reign curbed their power, drove many from his kingdom, and compelled the remainder to live at peace with his subjects.

Cormac and most of his Chiefs fell in battle, with Flann, head of the Southern Hy Nials, in the year 903, and the incursions of the Danes, now reinforced by many of their countrymen, became more fierce than ever. In 920 an expedition from Limerick sailed up the Shannon, laid waste and plundered Clonmacnois and Inis-Cealtra, or Holy Island in Lough Derg, ravaged the neighbourhood, and returned laden with great spoils. Contentions arose between the Danes of Dublin and Limerick, in which the latter were victorious. In 927 they took possession of Lough Corrib, whose shores they wasted; but shortly afterwards they suffered a defeat from the men of Connaught, near Lough Ree. In 931, under Amlav, the Danes of Limerick ravaged Galway, having defeated the Irish Chiefs with great slaughter. They traversed Connaught as far as Boyle in the next year, and there seemed to be no power in Ireland capable of opposing them. The rivalry which existed between the Monarchs of the North and South prevented any combination being effected; and not seldom one or other sought the assistance of the foreigners against his own rival.

In the year 942 the Danes suffered their first important defeat. A great annual fair was held which lasted fourteen days, and was attended by merchants from all parts of the country, and even from foreign parts. The Danes of Limerick, under Tomar, formed the project of attacking and plundering the merchants collected at the fair. Tomar was joined by his kinsmen of Connaught and Waterford, and all marched secretly into Ormond. The Irish however observed the hostile conjunction. The country was alarmed by fires on each hill top. The native forces collected together, and being reinforced by those attending the fair, fell on the Danes, whom they defeated with a loss of four thousand men. The men of Munster and Leinster joined their forces under Lorcan, grandfather of Brian Boru, fell upon the Danes and routed them with great slaughter on another occasion. Whenever a union was effected the Irish showed they were as valiant and as brave as their opponents.

In 945 Callachan, King of Cashel, succeeded in uniting most of the southern Chiefs in an attempt to strike a blow for the final deliverance of their countrymen. Limerick, as being the seat of the enemy's power, was selected as the point of attack. Having arrived with his forces within a short distance of the city, Callachan sent a summons to the Danes to surrender their stronghold, and give hostages for their future behaviour. To this demand the Northmen replied haughtily that they were more accustomed to receive hostages than to give them, and that so far from surrendering, or even waiting to be attacked, they would march out from their fortress and give him battle before its walls. And so they did. Amlav divided his troops into four divisions, and joined battle with the Munster Monarch on the hills of Singland. The contest was a fierce and bloody one, and for a long time

ST SAVIOUR'S DOMINICAN CHURCH. LIMERICK. MESSᴿˢ GOLDIE & CHILD ARCHᵀˢ

success was doubtful. At length Callachan singled out the Danish Chief for single contest. With one mighty blow the Monarch cleft the Viking to the chin, through helmet and skull. In like manner 'the tall, graceful chief, O'Sullivan', with one stroke of his sword cut off the head of Moran, son of the King of Denmark, and the lifeless trunk fell at his feet. Other Danish chiefs fell in single battle – O'Keeffe running his spear through the body of the Standard Bearer. The Danes now gave way on all sides dismayed at the loss of their leaders. They fled to the city, followed by the Irish, who put two thousand to the sword during the pursuit.

Callachan permitted the Danes to remain in possession of the city in the enjoyment of their own laws and subject to their own chiefs, contenting himself with merely taking hostages and exacting large contributions. It is a strange sequel to the victory to learn that shortly afterwards, in 951, the Danes of Limerick and the men of Munster united in again ravaging Clonmacnois.

Soon, however, an avenger arose, who crushed and almost annihilated the power of these rapacious foreigners. The Dalcassians, under Mahon, were now coming into prominence and asserting their superiority. In 969, the Dalcassians, headed by Mahon, King of Cashel, and his brother, Brian Boru, encountered the Danes under Ivar at Sollohed, within a short distance of the present Limerick Junction. Victory declared in favour of the gallant brothers, and the raven flag of the Northmen drooped in flight. Three thousand were slain in battle, and the remainder fled to Limerick. The city was attacked, plundered and burned to the ground, and its rich spoils became the booty of the Munster troops.

An interesting glimpse is afforded of the wealth and trade of the Danish colony in Limerick in the 10th century, by the following extract:

They [the victors of Sulcoit] carried off their jewels and their best property and their saddles beautiful and foreign; their gold and their silver; their beautifully-woven cloth of all colours and of all kinds; their satin and their silken cloth pleasing and variegated, both scarlet and green, and all sorts of cloths in like manner. They carried away their soft youthful bright matchless girls, their blooming silk-clad young women, and their active, large and well formed boys.

Even so far back as the 10th century we read of the 'bright matchless girls' of Limerick.

Though defeated here the Danes were victorious elsewhere, and fresh hordes arriving, the city rose from its ashes again to become more formidable. In 973, reinforced by the men of the Orkneys, they seized Scattery Island, which they plundered, converting it into an arsenal. They formed alliances with the Eugenians, the hereditary rivals of the Dalcassians. But in vain. In 975 they were again defeated by Mahon and Brian. Mahon was shortly after betrayed by O'Donovan and put to death; but this only hastened the doom of the Northmen. Brian, who succeeded to the vacant throne, attacked Scattery, slew Ivar and his two sons, and slaughtered the garrison, to the number of eight hundred. Limerick was taken and burned and the Northmen compelled to submit. He spared their lives; but they had to pay tribute. In the course of time they lost their identity, and gradually amalgamated with those amongst whom they had taken up their abode. Brian carried his arms elsewhere. Victory after victory rested upon his banners. He broke the power of the Northmen in no less than forty battles; nor did he rest, till on Good Friday, in the year 1014, by the battle of Clontarf, he achieved the national deliverance, sealing the conquest with his blood.

CHAPTER II

Limerick Under
The O'Briens

ALTHOUGH FOREIGN FOES WERE QUELLED, yet Munster, and particularly Limerick, was not allowed to enjoy the long unknown blessings of peace and tranquillity. Death had removed the only man capable of raising the petty Kings and Princes above their trivial feuds, and uniting them in a national confederation. No sooner was the brave Brian laid in his grave – full of years and full of honours – than an unnatural feud arose between his two surviving sons, Teige and Donogh. During the miserable years of the fratricidal struggle the city was the prey, now of one faction now of the other, according as the one or the other gained some slight advantage. The unhappy town learned by sad experience that there were others as cruel and as destructive as the Danes. At length, after some years of civil war, Teige was found murdered, and the suspicion was rife that Donogh (O'Brien) instigated the bloody deed in hope of getting his dominions. Teige, however, left a son, Turlogh, who succeeded to the vacant throne, in which he had the support of Diarmid, King of Leinster, son-in-law of Donogh. Turlogh and Diarmid invaded the territory of the latter, and stormed Limerick. Many engagements took place between the relatives, till at last Diarmid, after ravaging the County of Limerick, defeated Donogh in a great battle in the Glen of Aherlow. Turlogh again defeated his kinsman in 1063, and reduced Limerick to ashes. Overwhelmed by repeated misfortunes, Donogh at last submitted to his fate, resigned his crown, and spent the remainder of his days in monastic seclusion at Rome.

Turlogh, the grandson of Brian Boru, died in 1086, and was succeeded in the Kingdom of Thomond by his son Murtagh. This Monarch levied war against Donald MacLaughlin, who claimed the chief sovereignty of Ireland as head of the Hy Nials, and for twenty years hostilities raged between the North and South. In revenge for the burning of Kincora, Murtagh led his Dalcassians into Ulster and demolished Aileach, the celebrated palace of his rival. He ordered his soldiers to carry the very stones to Limerick, and with them built a parapet on his own royal residence, situated where St. Mary's Cathedral now stands. Murtagh died in 1119, and was the last of his family who held the supreme power bequeathed to them by Brian Boru. Henceforth the O'Briens were simply Kings of Thomond, and as Limerick was their chief seat, their dominion was generally called the Kingdom of Limerick.

The reigns of the subsequent Monarchs were feeble in the extreme, powerless for good, and a savage scene of conflict and rebellion. At last an able and capable leader appeared in Donald, who came to the throne in 1164. He was a brave soldier, a firm ruler, and under him Limerick enjoyed some peace and quietness. But this happy state of things was to be of short duration. A mighty change was impending. A new and formidable power appeared on the troubled scene of Irish political history, before which the independence of her Kings and Princes melted away and finally disappeared.

In 1169 the first party of Norman adventurers landed in Waterford at the invitation of Dermot, King of Leinster. The Irish seem to have been paralysed by this unexpected danger. The local feuds of centuries had borne their bitter fruit. Split up into rival bands and factions they could not unite even in the face of this terrible foe. The brilliant tactics – the glittering armour – the long shining spears – the close serried ranks of the Norman Knights – struck terror into a people who had met no warlike enemies since Clontarf, one hundred and fifty years before. In a short time the Normans made themselves masters of the kingdom, and Henry II on his arrival found he had only to receive the submission of numerous Chieftains. Amongst the first who attended to do homage at Cashel was Donald, King of Limerick. He consented to surrender the city to Henry, and hold his kingdom

Thomondgate Bridge.

as a fief from the English King.

Donald's somewhat hasty submission is only to be explained by the usual jealousy. Roderick O'Connor, King of all Ireland, belonged to the family which fifty years before wrested the Sceptre from the degenerate Kings of Thomond. Hence the unnecessary haste. No sooner however had the English King departed than Donald saw the consequence of his act, renounced his allegiance, and drove the English from Limerick. Strongbow himself advanced to crush a revolt which threatened to become general. The English, assisted by the Danes of Dublin, had proceeded as far as Thurles, when Donald and his Dalcassians fell upon them, and by a vigorous night attack almost annihilated the whole expedition. Strongbow fled from the field and shut himself up in Waterford.

In the following year, 1175, Raymond le Gros, one of the ablest of the English generals, was despatched with an army to recover possession of the city. They arrived without meeting any opposition at the banks of the Shannon, which then completely encompassed the city. It was the month of October. The stream was rapid and swollen from recent rains. All the bridges had been broken down. For a time the invaders stood irresolute, looking at the city and the river, not knowing what to do. Whilst the leaders were considering the expediency of effecting a retreat, Raymond's nephew and a common soldier spurred into the river to ascertain whether it was fordable or not. Both succeeded in crossing to the King's Island; but in returning the soldier was swept away by the current and drowned. Another nephew, Meyler Fitzhenry, undeterred by the manifest danger, plunged into the river, succeeded in crossing, and soon stood on the opposite shore, protecting himself with his shield from the showers of stones and arrows cast at him from the walls. Raymond, seeing the peril to which his favourite nephew was exposed, called upon his army to follow him, and shouting his battle cry, hastened to his support. The whole army crossed with the loss of only a few. The Irish, who considered themselves safe, were thunderstruck at the daring and unexpected nature of the attack, and fled in dismay. They were pursued into the city with great slaughter and the place fell into the hands of the English.

Raymond's popularity with the army and his recent brilliant success excited the jealousy of some of the Norman nobles, and he was summoned on frivolous charges to appear before the King. On his departure Donald appeared before the walls, and so closely invested[1] the place that the English army within the city were in danger of perishing by famine. An expedition for their relief was organised; but the soldiers refused to march under any other leader than Raymond. Raymond was therefore recalled and placed in command, and moreover had the assistance of the King of Ossory and his Irish subjects. On hearing of the approach of the Norman and Irish forces, Donald raised the siege and entrenched himself near Cashel, there to await the arrival of his foes. A long and obstinate engagement took place. The Dalcassians were animated with the remembrance of the victory gained near that spot two years before. The English fought with the courage of despair, for they knew that if once the tide of victory turned against them their own Irish allies would complete their destruction. At length victory decided for Raymond, and Donald's troops were routed with great slaughter.

The brave Monarch, convinced at last of the hopelessness of fighting singlehanded against the English, and seeing Irishmen deserting the national flag for that of their enemies, gave up the hopeless task. He surrendered to Raymond, renewed his engagements to Henry, and gave hostages for his future allegiance.

Again a change occurred which gave Donald an opportunity of recovering his kingdom and asserting his independence. Earl Strongbow died in Dublin, and Raymond, who was his brother-in-law, was recalled with the army to secure Leinster and the Capital. Before setting out, he entrusted the city to Donald, to be held for the English King, reminding him of his recent allegiance, and that he was now one of Henry's barons. Raymond had no sooner departed from the city than the bridges were broken down, the whole place burned to the ground – Donald vowing it should never again become a nest for foreigners.

Owing to various causes the English hold upon the Island was gradually becoming weaker; and in order to recover some of the

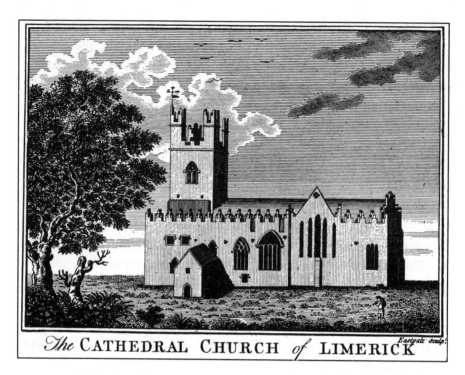

The CATHEDRAL CHURCH *of* LIMERICK

*St Mary's Cathedral – Donal Mor O'Brien (last King of Munster)
commissioned its building in 1168.*

ground which had been lost, Henry conferred on his youngest son, John, the title of Lord of Ireland, and appointed De Lacy Chief Governor. The Kingdom of Limerick was bestowed upon two noblemen who declined the gift. It was then granted to Philip de Braosa, with the exception of the city, which was reserved to the King and his heirs. Braosa collected an army and departed to take possession of his new dominions. He had no confidence in his followers, and foreseeing an obstinate and perhaps successful defence on the part of the men of Limerick, Braosa gave up the enterprise and left the country.

In 1185 Henry sent over his son, John, as Chief Governor of Ireland, accompanied by a large army and a rapacious crowd of adventurers, eager to enrich themselves at the expense of the inhabitants. Many of the native Chiefs flocked to do homage to the young Prince, but the foolish conduct of the youth, and the insolence of the Norman nobles so roused their indignation, that preparations were made for a general revolt. Matters now became so serious that it seemed as if the end of English power in Ireland was not far off, and John was recalled in haste. But the dissensions of the native Chiefs again laid the country at the mercy of the invaders, and to add to the national distress, King Donald died in 1194, and now there was no capable leader left in Ireland. During his long reign of twenty-six years the English found in the King of Thomond their ablest and most successful opponent. Had his countrymen seconded his efforts instead of arraying themselves under the banner of St. George, the so-called conquest might have been delayed till much later times. Donald was by far the most remarkable leader of his time in Ireland. He was an astute statesman – an able ruler – a brave soldier. If he was rather brisk in submitting to Henry II and just as ready to renounce his allegiance as opportunity served, it must be borne in mind that submission did not mean much on either side, and that the King of Thomond was not the only offender in that respect. Donald is memorable also for his munificent gifts to the church. Numerous abbeys owe their foundation to him. He erected the Cathedral of Killaloe, and within its walls he was buried. He founded St. Mary's Cathedral, bestowing his own palace

The River Shannon as seen from Thomond Bridge.

for the site, and endowing the Church with ample grants.

In the confusion that followed upon the death of Donald the English got possession of Limerick. John, on his accession to the throne five years after, renewed his father's grant of Thomond to Braosa, and committed the custody of the city to William de Burgho. From this date onward for upwards of four hundred years Limerick remained exclusively English. The Kingdom of Thomond, or Limerick, existed but in name. The seat of sovereignty was transferred to Clonroad, near Ennis, and the connection of the O'Brien dynasty with Limerick, their former seat of power, gradually ceased. The Charter of Limerick dates from 1197, granting the citizens power to choose a Mayor and two Bailiffs, to whose hands its government was entrusted.

In 1210 King John resolved on visiting Ireland for the purpose of restoring order if possible. During his stay the conquered portions were divided into twelve counties, Limerick being one of them. He visited the city during his sojourn and was greatly pleased with its situation. He erected the castle which still bears his name, and caused Thomond Bridge to be built, a structure which lasted down to the year 1838. King John's was the only visit ever paid by an English Monarch to Limerick. Large numbers of English now flocked to the city and made it their residence. During all the troubles of the next three centuries Limerick remained loyal to the cause of England, and was undisturbed by the terrible commotions which raged up to its very gates. During this long period only a few incidents deserve notice.

In 1316 Edward Bruce entered Limerick on the 21st of September, and held his court there till the following Easter. The gallant Scot endeavoured to win a kingdom for himself as his brother did at Bannockburn. He was crowned King of Ireland at Dundalk, and many Irish and English nobles joined his train. The enterprise was not successful. On the arrival of Sir Roger Mortimer, the Justiciary, and fearing a hostile coalition of the Anglo-Irish nobles, he moved northward. His little army was wasted with famine and pestilence, and in 1318, near Dundalk, was completely routed by Bermingham, and Bruce himself was amongst the slain.

In 1331 a number of the followers of the Earl of Desmond, who had been imprisoned in the castle, suddenly overpowered their guards and seized possession of the fortress, putting the constable to the sword. The citizens, under Bamberry, the Mayor, soon recovered possession of the place, and to avenge the constable's murder, put all the prisoners to death.

In 1483, Gerald, Earl of Kildare, Chief Governor of Ireland, held a Parliament in Limerick; but no record of its proceedings or enactments has been preserved.

In the subsequent century nothing worthy of record is to be found. Even during the long Desmond wars in the reign of Elizabeth, the chief transactions of which took place in the County of Limerick, the name of the city only occurs in connection with the arrival and departure of troops, or the execution of some prominent Chief, whose rank entitled him to the formalities of a trial.

CHAPTER III

Limerick – 1641-1651

IT IS ENTIRELY OUTSIDE THE SCOPE of the present work to attempt to describe the various causes which led to the slaughter and insurrection of 1641. Suffice it to say that the misery of the greater mass of the population, the grinding tyranny of Strafford, and the weakness of the royal cause, produced their natural results. A plot was formed, chiefly at the instigation of Rory O'More, the object of which was to seize Dublin, expel the English, and restore the Irish to lands which had been formerly theirs. The attempt on Dublin failed; but in the North the Irish rose in a mass against the English settlers. It is difficult now to arrive at an exact knowledge of what did actually take place at that time, both in Ulster and in other parts of the kingdom, especially as the vast mass of evidence that has come down to us is practically unworthy of credit, according to modern notions of evidence. In England the King and the Parliament were too busily engaged over their own quarrels to bestow much attention upon the affairs of Ireland, which were to some extent left to adjust themselves.

Early in the movement, the confederates, having obtained possession of Kilkenny and Waterford, marched on Limerick, for whose security no provision had been made. The citizens opened the gates and received the Irish army with open arms. For the first time for four hundred years Limerick ceased to own allegiance to England. Only the garrison in the castle refused to admit the insurgents. Captain Courtenay, relying on help from England, which never came, determined to hold out to the last. He had but sixty regular soldiers under his command; but with auxiliaries and others could muster two hundred men. The supply of ammunition was small, and to make matters worse, the garrison was sorely in want of provisions.

The Irish army at once adopted rigorous measures to reduce the castle. In order to cut off all chance of relief from the side of the river, a great boom was thrown across from one bank to the other. The boom was formed of trunks of trees bound securely together by iron bolts. One end was fastened to the quay tower, near where the Courthouse now stands, the other was made secure to huge piles of stonework on the site of the present Strand Barracks. It was not without loss that it was constructed and placed in position, for the castle guns kept up a well-sustained fire. At the same time offensive operations were not neglected. A gun was mounted upon the Cathedral tower, from which a cannonade was opened on the castle; but the walls were stronger than was thought, and the resistance more effective than had been anticipated by the besiegers.

More expeditious efforts were necessary, and it was now resolved to undermine the walls, and thus expose the defences. Large excavations were made under the outer wall of the castle, on the side facing the Cathedral, which was the weakest part of the fortress. These excavations were roofed and propped up with dry timber, smeared with tar and other combustible matter. At a given signal the woodwork was set on fire, and being rapidly consumed, the roof of the cavern fell in, carrying down with it a large extent of the wall, and a wide breach was thus made. Courtenay seeing he could no longer maintain possession of his post capitulated on honourable terms, and the castle, ammunition, and guns fell into the hands of the Irish. The great gun on the platform next to the town was described as being so large that it required thirty-five yoke of oxen to draw it. The captured cannon were employed in reducing the various strongholds in the neighbourhood from which still floated the English flag.

Up to then the insurgents seem to have acted from impulse; but the organization was now completed by the general assembly at Kilkenny in October, 1642. Eleven spiritual peers, fourteen temporal, and two hundred commoners, represented the Roman Catholics of Ireland. The executive government was entrusted to a supreme council, with Lord Mountgarret as its president. A great seal was ordered to be

THE CITTIE OF LIMERICK

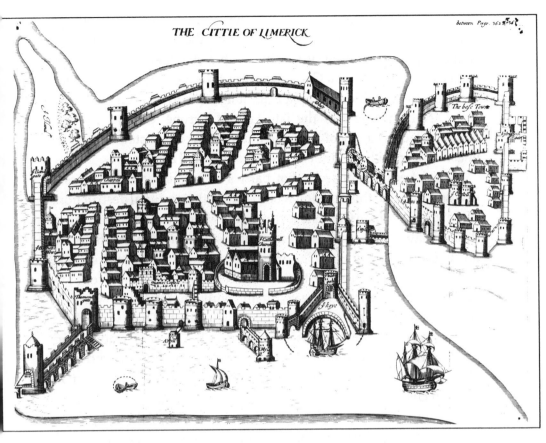

Map of Limerick from an 1820 edition of the Pacata Hibernia.

made, a new coinage was issued, a levy of thirty thousand soldiers was ordered, and finally a remonstrance to the King was drawn up, containing a declaration of loyalty, with a statement of grievances under which the Roman Catholics were suffering, and a petition for their redress. An able and capable military leader was found in Owen Roe O'Neill, nephew of the late Earl of Tyrone. Colonel Preston commanded the army of Leinster, and both were assisted by experienced officers, who had served with continental armies.

It soon became apparent that parties in Ireland were hopelessly divided, and that this division would lead to their mutual destruction. The extreme Roman Catholic section were willing to help Charles, but desired national independence and the restoration of their religion to all its former splendour. The moderate men attached to the royal cause and equally anxious to see their religion once more predominant, did not desire to break finally with England, and were in constant communication with the English Royalists. There was a third party – the Protestant Royalists – headed by the Earl of Ormond, and yet a fourth, hostile to Protestant Episcopacy, Catholicism, and Royalty – the rising Puritan party – represented by Munro and the Scottish army in Ulster.

The only hope for all parties was a union under the Lord Lieutenant, and a temporary arrangement of this kind was eventually effected by the moderate men of the three prominent sections. In 1645 Rinuccini, the Papal Legate, arrived with a supply of arms and money, and vigorously denounced the recent arrangement with Ormond. Ormond and the commissioners of the supreme council agreed to a cessation of hostilities for one year; but the clergy would accept no compromise. An attempt to proclaim the peace in Limerick was received with violence. The Herald, attired in his coat of office, and attended by the Mayor and several Aldermen, began to read the proclamation at the market cross. The populace, headed by Alderman Fanning and Father Wolfe, a Dominican, made a furious attack upon the party. Such showers of stones were thrown upon the occasion that the anniversary for the day was popularly called Stoney Thursday. The Herald and Mayor, wounded and bleeding profusely, with difficulty escaped with their lives from the fury of the people, and no further attempt was made to proclaim the peace in Limerick. In consequence of his action on this occasion, the Mayor was deposed, and Alderman Fanning was elected by popular vote to fill the vacant post.

On the faith of some secret negotiations between Charles and the confederates, an Irish army was levied to assist the royal cause. But in the meantime the English Royalists had been utterly defeated at Naseby, and the King himself was a prisoner in the hands of the Scots. The Irish levies were therefore detained and sent to recover Bunratty Castle, which had fallen into the hands of a Parliamentary expedition. The post was a most important one; but the Irish troops failed to recover possession of it and were pursued to the very gates of Limerick. The supreme council determined to succeed at all hazards, and both they and the Papal Nuncio moved to Limerick in order to carry on operations with more vigour. After a siege of twelve days the Castle of Bunratty fell into their hands.

About the same time a splendid victory was gained in the northern provinces, O'Neill encountered Munro and the Scottish army at Benburb, on the Blackwater, near Armagh. The result was a crushing defeat of the Scots, who fled, leaving their camp, artillery, and baggage, in possession of the Irish leader. Thirty-two stand of colours were captured and sent to the Nuncio as a trophy of the victory. They reached Limerick on the 13th of June, 1646, a week after the battle. A magnificent demonstration was organised. The colours were carried in triumph through the streets to St. Mary's Cathedral, where a solemn *Te Deum* was chanted.

Soon however the result of the mutual animosities became apparent. Ormond delivered up Dublin to the Parliament and left the kingdom. Jones was appointed Governor, and marching out, defeated Preston and the Leinster army. Lord Inchiquin took Cashel by assault and put the inhabitants to the sword, and destroyed the Munster army under Taafe at Knockanos, near Kanturk. The Marquis of Ormond now returned to Ireland with power to treat with the supreme council. There were therefore two Royalist leaders, Ormond and O'Neill, and these two hated one another more cordially than either hated the Puritans. Ormond's overtures were accepted in spite of the bitter opposition of the Nuncio. The council and Inchiquin united their forces and marched to crush O'Neill. The Nuncio hurled the sentence of excommunication against the council and their forces, and laid an interdict on all places which should receive them. Seeing all his efforts in vain the Nuncio left Kilkenny, repaired to Galway, and departed from the kingdom, his mission having ended in failure. A peace was proclaimed between Ormond and the council; but too late. Before it could be ratified Charles's head had fallen on the scaffold, and Oliver Cromwell was Lord Lieutenant of Ireland.

Cromwell landed in Dublin on the 14th of August, 1649, bringing with him nine thousand foot, four thousand horse, and several pieces of artillery. On 31st of August he took the field with a large and well appointed army. Drogheda was taken by assault, and the garrison, largely composed of English Royalists put to the sword. He then turned southward. Wexford was betrayed, and the same promiscuous slaughter followed. Hugh O'Neill, nephew and successor to Owen O'Neill, who had died a few months previously, held Clonmel, with the Ulster army of his uncle, and prepared to resist to the last. In his first assault Cromwell was repulsed with great loss, so that he was compelled to turn the siege into a blockade. An Irish army advancing to the relief of Clonmel was defeated, and after a gallant defence O'Neill drew off his forces secretly to Waterford, and the town surrendered on honourable terms. Urgent affairs called Cromwell to England, and on his departure, the conduct of the campaign was entrusted to his son-in-law, General Ireton.

In spite of all their reverses, the Irish Royalists would still have been able to hold their own against any force that could be brought against them, if they would only agree to act in concert. The whole province of Connaught was theirs. The seaports of Limerick and Galway were in their hands. But they were divided, and therefore powerless. Even the dread presence of Cromwell could not fuse the heterogeneous elements into one compact whole. Limerick refused to accept a garrison for its defence offered by Ormond. To such an extent did the spirit

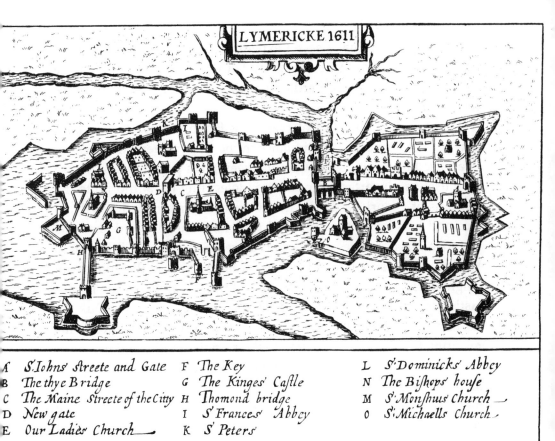

A	S. Iohns streete and Gate	F	The Key	L	S. Dominicks Abbey
B	The thye Bridge	G	The Kinges Castle	N	The Bishops house
C	The Maine streete of the Citty	H	Thomond bridge	M	S. Monshus Church
D	New gate	I	S. Frances Abbey	O	S. Michaells Church
E	Our Ladies Church	K	S. Peters		

Map of Limerick in 1611 from Speed's Maps of Irish Towns.

of faction prevail, that a secret expedition against the Parliamentarians was stopped on its march by Father Wolfe, who seized the colours, and denounced perdition against any one that should proceed further.

At last an open breach took place. The Bishops drew up a declaration against Ormond's continuance in the Government, threatening to accuse him to the King. Ormond seeing his presence was worse than useless, departed from Ireland, delegating his authority to the Marquis of Clanrickard. The new Governor was treated exactly as Ormond had been. He proposed to defend the city and share its fortunes. His overtures were promptly rejected, though Sir Hardress Waller, with a large body of cavalry, was hovering in the immediate neighbourhood. The Extremists wasted much valuable time in fantastic projects, and even entered into negotiations with the Duke of Lorraine, offering to invest him with royal powers on condition of his restoring the Church and nation to their original independence.

In the meantime Ireton directed all his energies to the complete subjugation of the Island. He sent for and received large reinforcements from England. Everything was in readiness, and as soon as the season opened, he resolved to strike a decisive blow by attacking Limerick, the centre of the enemy's position. The Irish troops under the Earl of Castlehaven, were encamped near Killaloe, along the Clare bank of the Shannon, in a strongly fortified position, defended by breastworks. Another large body under the Lord Lieutenant held possession of the western part of Connaught, and lay near Galway. The garrison of Limerick had been considerably strengthened, and was commanded by Hugh O'Neill, who in the previous year had so gallantly defended Clonmel against the Protector himself.

Every precaution was taken by Ireton in approaching the city. Kilmallock and Castle-Connell had been reduced. Early in the Spring the English army was drawn up at Cashel. From thence a strong detachment of four thousand men was sent into Connaught, by way of Sligo, so as to draw off the troops from the Shannon. Ireton himself advanced by way of Nenagh, the garrison of which surrendered on his approach. He then directed his march on Killaloe, and encamped on the left bank of the Shannon, in front of the Irish army, the two being separated only by the river. The English set themselves to lower the bank so as to widen the river, and thus make it fordable, and the Irish made every preparation to oppose their passage. But all this time the English general was searching the river southward, so as to discover a ford, and the required spot was pointed out to him by the treachery of an Irish officer. A road was secretly constructed through a morass to the ford which was at O'Brien's Bridge, and a favourable opportunity was all that was required to attempt the crossing.

The division under Coote, which had been sent into Connaught, accomplished its mission satisfactorily. Whilst pretending to lay siege to Sligo, Clanrickard and the Connaught army moved northward to save the place. Suddenly Coote gave them the slip, marched across the Curlew mountains, surprised and captured Athlone, and then moved on Galway. To save this important seaport, Castlehaven withdrew a large portion of his forces from the Shannon. This was the move that Ireton was waiting for. That night he directed three regiments of foot, one of horse, and four pieces of artillery to force the passage at O'Brien's Bridge. On arriving at the river, they found only two boats to carry them across. The first boatful seized an old castle on the opposite bank, but was compelled to give way, the Irish coming to the attack. Reinforcements arrived, but a brisk cannonade compelled the Irish to retire from the bank behind some rising ground, and the whole body crossed in safety. Colonel Fennell, who had been left in charge at Killaloe, deserted his post, either through cowardice or treachery, and fled to Limerick. In any case his remaining was useless after the detachment crossed at O'Brien's Bridge. About this time also an English fleet appeared in the Shannon, bringing ammunition and supplies. Thus the whole river was in the hands of the Parliamentarians.

CHAPTER IV

Siege by Ireton

EARLY IN APRIL, 1651, Ireton marched on Limerick, without encountering any resistance. In the middle of the Shannon, on the great Lax Weir, just above the city, there still stands a small square tower, which at the time was occupied by a small body of Irish. Colonel Tuthill, with two guns, was told off to take possession of it. The guns opened a brisk fire from the Clare side, near St. Patrick's Church, and the place became no longer tenable. The garrison took to their boats in order to join the main body at Limerick. The fire of the guns was now directed to the boats, and the men were compelled to surrender. Some landed at Parteen, and were put to the sword in defiance of all laws of civilized warfare. The indignation of Ireton was roused by the proceeding. Tuthill and his second in command, were tried by court martial and dismissed from the service. Those who were fortunate enough to land at Corbally were well treated and sent to headquarters uninjured.

The citizens of Limerick had made every preparation for a prolonged and obstinate resistance. The fortifications, which were of great strength, had been put in a thorough state of defence. The further end of Thomond Bridge was defended by a strong fort. At the city end was a drawbridge which could cut off communication at will. There also was King John's Castle, whose guns swept the bridge and commanded the approaches on the opposite side. The only possible way in which the city could be assaulted was by landing a force on the King's Island, a course which was extremely perilous. Ammunition was in abundance, and there were provisions for twelve months at least within the walls. To counterbalance these great advantages,

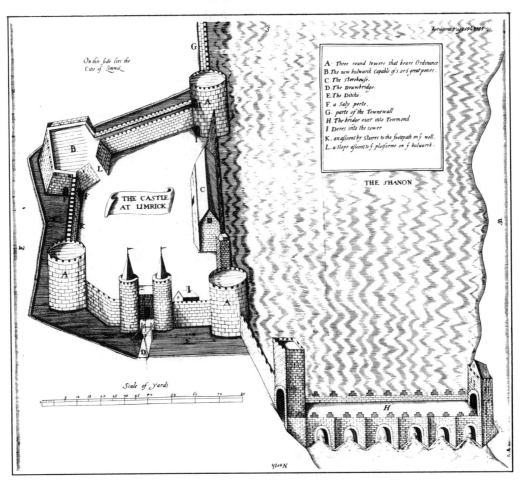

King John's Castle – a detail from the Pacata Hibernia.

the city was divided against itself. One party was anxious to come to an arrangement with Ireton almost on any terms. Others were determined to fight to the bitter end and defend the place to the last stone of the fortifications. It was also more than suspected that there were traitors within, ready to sell the place to the Parliamentary general. No assistance could be hoped for from without. Lord Muskerry had raised a body of troops in the South, but these were defeated with great loss by Lord Boghill. About the same time, Conor O'Brien and two thousand men of Clare were driven back by Ludlow. In the great struggle which was about to take place, Limerick had to maintain the fight alone and unsustained.

Upon the arrival of the English forces before the city, a formal summons from Ireton to surrender was indignantly rejected. Negotiations for a treaty were however commenced, and six commissioners were nominated from each side to arrange preliminaries. Several days were spent in deliberation. The Irish, aware of their strength, insisted on getting better terms than Ireton was willing to grant, and the conference broke up without anything being effected, and hostilities immediately commenced.

The first attempt was made on the fort at the Clare end of Thomond Bridge. A battery was erected, which played upon it with such effect that a breach was made in its walls and its guns silenced. A grand assault was then planned and carried into execution. A forlorn hope of twenty men, under the command of Captain Hackett, advanced cautiously and rapidly. They came to the breach, threw in their grenades, dashed in, headed by their commander and followed by a regiment of infantry, only to find the place deserted. The Irish had retired into the city, breaking down two arches of the bridge to prevent pursuit. In the vaults were discovered several barrels of gunpowder, with lighted matches by them, ready to blow up the place and all it contained. The new acquisition was found to be of no use, for it was commanded by the guns of the castle, and it would be impossible to repair the bridge in the face of the fire that could be directed upon it from the walls.

The next effort to capture the city was made on the side of the King's

Island. Three hundred men under Colonel Walker dropped down the river at midnight, and having effected a landing on the swampy bank, marched towards the outworks of the fortifications. Here they were met with a resistance such as they were not prepared to encounter. The Irish sallied from their trenches and attacked them with such impetuosity that they were all either driven into the river or put to the sword – the leader himself falling in the fight.

The complete failure of these two attempts convinced Ireton that it was useless to attempt to surprise the garrison or take the city by assault. He therefore made preparations for turning the siege into a blockade, waiting for sedition and treachery to effect what force of arms could not accomplish. A bridge was now constructed over the river, across which he conducted the greater part of his troops, forming them into a great fortified camp of six thousand men in three divisions, so as to surround the city. A large fort was constructed at the northern extremity of the King's Island, which was held by a thousand foot and three hundred horse under the command of Sir Hardress Waller.

The city was now completely hemmed in on all sides, and a tiresome and monotonous blockade began. During the long Summer days the two armies watched one another wearily, almost without an incident to vary the sameness of their inactivity. Within the walls the state of affairs was gradually becoming more and more deplorable, as time dragged on. The plague which had appeared in the country during the past few years began to rage amongst the inhabitants with great violence. In every street and alley its victims could be numbered by scores. The young and strong as well as the old and feeble were swept away by the terrible scourge. Those who survived moved about wan and meagre, more like skeletons than human beings. The very winds of heaven carried contagion in their breath, and the sun himself poured down his blazing beams into courts and alleys crowded with suffering creatures and reeking with deadly exhalations. During the Summer months the pale spectres of pestilence and death stalked through the city striking down their victims. Many endeavoured to fly through the lines of the enemy, but were driven back. It is related

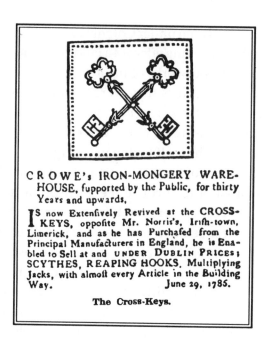

An 18th-century advertisement.

by Ludlow that a father and daughter were detected in the act of escaping, and the daughter was condemned to death. The old man implored that her life should be spared, and that he might be permitted to suffer in her stead. The request was denied. The girl was led to execution, and the father driven back into the city.

The besieging army was also in a no less perilous position. The supply of provisions – never very abundant – began to fail. On one occasion, Ireton was compelled to go in one direction and Ludlow in another, to scour the country in search of provisions. During their absence the watchful O'Neill sallied out at the head of two thousand men, and very nearly brought the siege to an abrupt termination. The English horseguard were surprised, and would have been overwhelmed but for the promptness of the infantry in coming to their assistance. Ireton speedily returned to keep a better watch over the garrison for the future. Ludlow remained to capture Clare Castle, but after an unsuccessful attempt rejoined his commander. Ague and fever thinned the English ranks, and gloom and despondency brooded over their camp. The forced inactivity was intolerable to men accustomed to the stirring scenes of battle, the dashing charge and the wild pursuit. They possessed one advantage conspicuously wanting in their opponents. They were united to a man.

Parties within the city could not lay aside their jealousies. Even the common misery increased the separation, and sharpened mutual animosities. The brave O'Neill, though Governor of the city, was such only in name, and was continually over-ruled and thwarted by the Mayor and magistracy. A numerous party kept up a secret correspondence with Ireton, and informed him of the state of affairs within. But O'Dwyer, Bishop of Limerick, and O'Brien, Bishop of Emly, and the ecclesiastics generally, would not hear of surrender on any terms. They animated the sinking spirits of the townsmen, exhorting them not to despair of ultimate success. The Summer had now passed into Autumn, and the Winter was fast approaching with its rains and floods. In a short time Ireton must break up his camp and depart into Winter quarters. There was no immediate danger of famine, for the garrison had provisions to last for the next four months at least, and

*An 18th-century advertisement for
Ryan's Muslin Warehouse.*

could they hold out a little longer the hostile forces must remove and leave the city untouched.

The English generals had formed a despondent view of the situation, and began to press Ireton to abandon what seemed to them a hopeless project. But Ireton knew it was not hopeless, for the traitors within would do his work in time. He issued a proclamation, threatening with death all who were not favourable to a speedy surrender, and even mentioned by name twenty-four persons whom he exempted from all hope of mercy. Amongst these were the two Prelates already mentioned, Father Wolfe, Alderman Fanning, and Hugh O'Neill.

The English general, in order to keep his army occupied, resolved upon a final assault. The weakest point of the defence was pointed out to him by an Irish officer. A battery was formed opposite that part of the wall. The great guns were conveyed thither from the ships and placed in position. A furious cannonade was opened and a breach effected. A parley was then beaten from the walls, and commissioners were selected from each side to effect an accommodation. Further resistance was made impossible by the action of that Colonel Fennell, whose conduct at Killaloe has been already referred to. Fennell seized St. John's Gate and Tower, which he filled with his own followers, and sent word to O'Neill that he was acting on the authority of the Mayor, and with the approval of many of the citizens. He had the audacity even to turn the guns upon the city, declaring he would not quit that post till the garrison had surrendered.

The only terms that Ireton would grant were that the soldiers should lay down their arms, the officers being permitted to retain their swords, and the men allowed to march wherever they pleased. The inhabitants got three months to remove themselves and their goods to wheresoever they were directed to reside. The twenty-four persons already referred to were doomed to death.

The garrison and citizens were naturally indignant at the terms offered, and resolved to hold out at all hazards. Fennell in the meantime received two hundred English soldiers into St. John's Tower, and a second was garrisoned by his own creatures, so that further resistance was out of the question. The closing days of October saw Ireton in possession of Limerick, after a determined defence lasting six months. The garrison, to the number of 2,500, laid down their arms in St. Mary's Cathedral, and marched out, several dropping dead of the plague as they departed. O'Neill met Ireton at the gates of the city, and informed him that several persons of the twenty-four, himself included, had submitted to his mercy, but he was at once placed under arrest. A few of the intended victims had escaped during the departure of the soldiery, one of them being the Bishop of Limerick. The Bishop of Emly, Father Wolfe, and General Purcell, were discovered in the pest house, brought before Ireton, and ordered to instant execution. Purcell begged hard for his life, and was so unmanned that he had to be supported to the place of execution. Not so the other two. The Bishop and Wolfe met their fate with courage and fortitude, and it is said O'Brien summoned Ireton to meet him within a year before a more awful tribunal.

Fanning managed to escape, but returned to get some money which he had secreted. His wife refused to receive him, and for some days he concealed himself in his ancestors' tomb in the Dominican Abbey. The cold was intense, and at length he crept shivering to the warmth of a guard fire. A former servant of his recognized him by the firelight and denounced him to the guard. The soldiers, by no means desirous of capturing the unhappy man, gave him time to escape. He was either unable or unwilling to stir, and was accordingly seized, brought before a court martial, and sentenced to death, but not before the soldiers plunged their swords into the body of the wretch who betrayed him. A greater traitor than he also met his doom. Fennell was shortly afterwards sentenced to death for murders he had committed in the early years of the insurrection.

O'Neill was tried before a court martial, and pleaded in his defence that the war had been several years on foot before he accepted the command of an Irish army; that he had nothing to do with the scenes of 1641 – being at that time on the continent – that he had acted as a fair and honourable opponent, and had faithfully observed the terms of the capitulation, much as he had disapproved of them. According to one account, the Puritan leader urged his condemnation for the blood spilt at Clonmel, and O'Neill was condemned to die. But such was the tempest of disapproval raised in the English army by both officers and men, that the odious sentence was cancelled, and a second trial acquitted O'Neill. There is another and far more probable story, that Ireton received O'Neill with the respect due to his valour, and set a guard over him only in order to ensure his safety, that when he felt the hand of death upon him subsequently, he commended O'Neill to the attention of Ludlow, and even requested that he might be one of those selected to convey his body to England, and as a matter of fact was present at Ireton's interment in Westminster Abbey. Sir Hardress Waller was made Governor of Limerick, the few detached garrisons still in possession of the Irish surrendered, amongst the last to capitulate being Colonel Grace, a descendant of Raymond le Gros, whose name will occur again.

1633

CHAPTER V

Siege by William III— 1690

AFTER THE BATTLE OF THE BOYNE, and the rapid flight of King James to France, the Irish army passed through Dublin, and retired westward behind the Shannon, still retaining possession of Athlone and Limerick. In the latter city the Duke of Tyrconnell held his viceregal court. William marched southward, by Kilkenny and Waterford, which he secured. Youghal surrendered early in August, and William directed his march to the Shannon. Limerick was thus again the point to which all eyes were turned, and on its garrison and citizens depended the fate of a dynasty.

Since the previous siege, forty years before, the fortifications of the city had been greatly strengthened. The Irish army, to the number of twenty thousand, lay on the right bank of the Shannon, guarding every important post. They had been fortunately relieved of the presence of their continental auxiliaries. Lauzun, when he saw Limerick, pronounced it to be untenable, adding that it was unnecessary to bring artillery against the walls, for they could be battered down with roasted apples. The French departed to Galway, there to await the transports which were to convey them to their own country.

King William determined to lose no time in endeavouring to secure possession of Limerick, now the most important post in Ireland. As he said himself, he came with the intention of not letting the grass grow under his feet. He sent three regiments of horse and two of dragoons, under Douglas, against Athlone, whilst with the main body of his army he marched more slowly against Limerick. Athlone was defended by a gallant soldier, Colonel Grace, a veteran who had seen service against the Parliamentarians. He was determined to hold out to the last, and said he – 'when my provisions are consumed I will eat my boots' before surrender. A hasty attempt by Douglas to storm Athlone was repulsed with the loss of four hundred men, and on being informed that Sarsfield was hurrying up, that incapable general retired in the night, and rejoined the main body.

The English troops were advancing by way of Carrick-on-Suir and Golden Bridge, and the 7th of August found them at Cahirconlish. King William had with him about twenty thousand men, and a field train of light artillery. The regular siege guns, consisting of six twenty-four pounders and two eighteen pounders, were on their way from Cashel, and were daily expected in camp. William was under the impression that on his arrival the city would be delivered up to him. He knew that the French had ignominiously deserted their allies, and that many, including Tyrconnell, were in favour of a capitulation. On his part he was willing to grant easy terms, so as to bring the campaign to a speedy conclusion, especially as his presence was wanted in England.

The Irish were better prepared to meet him than William expected. O'Brien's Bridge had been broken down. Strong bodies occupied entrenched positions at Killaloe and the ford of Annabeg. The approaches to the city were very difficult on all sides. The immediate neighbourhood was marshy, and intersected with deep trenches. The ground was almost impassable, owing to the recent rains, and the consequent flooding of the Shannon, and its little tributary, the Groody. The roads were narrow, difficult to traverse, and lined with hedges, behind which a large force could be concealed.

The City of Limerick possessed an able Governor in Boiseleau, a Frenchman. The Duke of Berwick and Wauchop were also good soldiers. But the animating spirit of the defenders was Patrick Sarsfield, a young colonel of dragoons. Sarsfield was descended from an Anglo-Norman family of distinction, one of whose early members was Standard Bearer to Henry II, and in more recent times another was Viscount Kilmallock, and premier Baronet of Ireland. The military career of Sarsfield commenced at an early age. He served as an ensign in Monmouth's regiment in France, and afterwards received his commission as lieutenant in the English Guards. By the death of his eldest brother, he inherited the family estate near Lucan, which produced a considerable income. He retired to France in 1688 with James, and accompanied that Monarch to Ireland in the subsequent year, when he was made colonel of the King's Dragoons. He was with the army at the Battle of the Boyne, but took no active part in the engagement, being ordered by the King to escort him to the left, where no fighting took place. His comment on James's conduct both during and after the engagement is well known – 'Change commanders, and we will fight the battle over again.' Sarsfield was now in the prime of life. In person he was tall, well made, and graceful in his carriage. His face was handsome, and bore the impress of every noble and manly quality. He was adored by the army, not only for his splendid military abilities, but for his genuine simplicity of character, transparent honesty, and disinterested generosity.

On the 8th of August, William sent forward from Cahirconlish an advanced guard of nine hundred men, to feel the strength of the Irish, and report upon their position. They advanced to within a short distance of the lines, and approached so near that the voices of the outposts were audible from one to the other. On the evening of the same day William made a personal inspection of the ground to be traversed by the army, and viewed the city from a distance. That night a council of war was summoned, and it was then decided to begin the march immediately, and to do so in order of battle.

At daylight, on the morning of the 9th of August, the camp at Cahirconlish was broken up, and the English forces advanced towards the city. A thousand foot and two hundred horse led the van, and pioneers in front levelled the ditches and filled up the drains. The Irish who were watching the enemy's movements, kept falling back in good order, their numbers being too small to risk an attack. At length they halted a short distance from the walls, determined to interrupt the advance. The position they had chosen was a strong one. The road in front was narrow and difficult, bounded on each side by a morass. Three roads led directly to the gates from where they stood. The central one, which was the broadest, was occupied by the Irish horse, the others were filled with infantry, and protected by the ditches.

When William saw that his opponents were determined to make a stand, and knowing that neither his infantry nor his cavalry could force the position, he brought up two field pieces, which opened fire beyond the range of the muskets. The Irish had no artillery to silence these guns, every shot from which fell amongst the masses of cavalry and at length compelled them to withdraw. The infantry were then attacked in a similar manner, and after a conflict which lasted two hours the place was evacuated. The Irish regiments retired, disputing every inch of the way, and took shelter under the walls. The English followed closely, and towards evening gained the semicircular range of hills at Singland. Before them lay the panorama of the city, at a distance of about five hundred yards, the intervening slopes covered with the retreating squadrons. An Irish redoubt[1] occupied the centre of the area, and behind this stretched the fortifications. The citadel at St. John's Gate was immediately in front defended by four towers. At the extreme left stood a tall tower, mounting three guns, and to the right frowned the well-known Black Battery. The walls at this point turned sharply towards Baal's Bridge, and in the centre was a sally-port. The bridge was exposed to view, but outside the range of the guns of the period. Conspicuous in the English town rose the square massive tower of St. Mary's Cathedral, from whose summit floated the standard of King James. To the extreme right, and without the walls, was the great fort constructed by Ireton, now by a curious change of circumstances, one of the most important of the defences, and the green sward of the King's Island was covered with the white tents of an Irish detachment.

As soon as the heads of the English columns appeared on the crest of the hills at Singland, every battery and fort on the long line of the fortifications opened a terrific fire, till the very earth trembled beneath the feet. The first to gain the heights were the Dutch Blue Guards, considered one of the finest regiments in Europe. They took possession of the elevation, and wheeling their field pieces into position, endeavoured to return the stern welcome they had received. The

Wellesley Bridge, now called Sarsfield Bridge.

Danish contingent to the right mounted four guns on a fort their ancestors had occupied, if not erected, many centuries before. On both sides the cannonading was kept up till darkness and fatigue put an end to further hostilities. The English army had been in motion since five o'clock in the morning, and it was not till eight in the evening that they were allowed to retire to their camp, which in the meantime had been pitched at Singland. William's activity that day was unceasing. He shared the toils and dangers of his soldiery, nor did he retire to rest till he had sent a troop of dragoons to try the ford at Annabeg.

These returned and reported that six regiments of foot, three of horse, and two of dragoons, were strongly entrenched on the opposite bank of the river.

Next morning a French deserter brought information to the city that William's heavy guns and ammunition were on their way from Cashel, escorted only by two troops of dragoons. Immediately it suggested itself to Sarsfield that here was a chance for cutting off and destroying the siege train. A little reflection showed that the project was within the bounds of possibility, and that it was the only chance of paralyzing the besieging army and saving the city for the present. It was such an undertaking, also, as commended itself to the fearless and dashing cavalry leader. Calling his troopers together he informed them of his design, pointing out the utility of the enterprise, at the same time not concealing from them the great danger that attended it. The gallant band volunteered for the work with enthusiasm, and that night saw them steal secretly out under the guidance of a bold rapparee[2] named Hogan, who knew every track and hiding place as well by night as by day. The strictest silence was preserved, and proceeding by the Clare bank of the Shannon they crossed the river a little above Killaloe at a place called Ballyvalley. The town and bridge were occupied by English soldiers; but so cautiously had the party proceeded that they passed over unobserved, and got into Tipperary in safety. Sarsfield then directed his route to Keeper Hill, and as the dawn was now approaching, halted his troopers safe from observation in the recesses of that mountainous district. When day was fully come, scouts were sent out in all directions who returned towards evening with the intelligence that the battering train was proceeding leisurely on its way, that the slender escort anticipated no danger, and were to encamp that night within the borders of the county, at Ballyneety, near an old castle.

Sarsfield's departure from Limerick, and his nocturnal march, had not escaped the observation of two Clare gentlemen who brought the information to the English camp. The generals did not consider the matter worthy of any attention; but not so the King, who divined at once that the secret expedition had for its object the destruction of his artillery. He ordered Sir John Lanier to take with him five hundred men and go to meet them. Lanier was rather dilatory in his movements, and looking upon his journey as unnecessary, did not set out till two o'clock in the morning, and arrived in time to be too late.

The train upon which so much depended, and which was an object of anxiety to both commanders, halted in the calm Summer's evening on a pleasant grassy plain, near the foot of a conical hill and close beside the castle of Ballyneety. The convoy being within twelve miles of the English army, anticipated no danger, and consequently omitted some of the usual precautions. The cannon and wagons were left in the order of march. The horses were allowed to graze about loosely tethered, and only a few sentinels were posted around the temporary halting place. By an odd coincidence the watchword for the night was 'Sarsfield'.

When the approach of evening rendered detection difficult, if not impossible, the Irish horse left their hiding place, and making a considerable circuit, got behind the convoy. They passed through the village of Cullen, lately vacated by the train, and moving with great rapidity, gained the summit of the hill which overlooked the sleeping camp. One of the scouts during the day had managed to ascertain the password, and by its aid the first sentinel was passed without any alarm being raised. The next sentry challenged, and one of the party shouting 'Sarsfield is the word and Sarsfield is the man', fired a pistol in his face. This was the appointed signal. The Irish now rushed to the attack with loud and exultant cries. The dragoons, suddenly roused from sleep, and confounded at the unexpected onslaught, could make no resistance. Some tried to catch their horses and were cut down, others were sabred where they lay. With the utmost despatch the guns were collected together, crammed with powder and placed upright with their muzzles in the ground, the ammunition and wagons were piled above and around in a huge heap and ignited. Soon a lurid flame shot heavenward, and a terrific explosion bursting on the silence of the night proclaimed to the distant camp and city that the siege train had been rendered totally useless.

As soon as it was seen that the expedition had succeeded beyond his wildest expectations, Sarsfield gathered his men around him and departed as rapidly as he came. Just then Lanier came up in time to see the last of the Irish disappearing in the gloom. Pursuit would be in vain but hoping to intercept the party yet, he wheeled to the left in order to cut off Sarsfield's retreat at Killaloe. But Sarsfield did not go by way of Killaloe. He rode northward to Banagher, and there crossed the Shannon, breaking down the bridge to prevent pursuit. He got back to Limerick without encountering any danger, and he and his gallant troops were received with the loudest acclamation by the citizens and their comrades in arms. The utmost joy pervaded the city, and the entire army did honour to the skill, secrecy, and daring with which the enterprise had been planned and executed. The midnight expedition saved Limerick for another year. It was a magnificent achievement and deserves to be classed amongst the most brilliant exploits of modern warfare.

Nothing daunted by the unexpected disaster, William still determined to push on operations as vigorously as possible whilst waiting for the arrival of a second siege train. As there was no time to be lost, on the very morning of Sarsfield's arrival in Limerick, Ginkle was sent with five thousand men to force the passage of the river. It was anticipated that the operation would be attended with difficulty and danger, both on account of the state of the river and the large body of horse on the opposite side. Ginkle marched along the Park road, toward Corbally, his army being all the time exposed to a galling flank fire from the battery near Baal's Bridge. A crossing was effected at a spot immediately above St. Thomas's Island which is said to have been pointed out by a fisherman named MacAdam. The Irish withdrew without striking a blow, and William had thus possession of both sides of the river.

On the 13th of August, Brigadier Stewart had despatched with four field pieces to capture Castle-Connell, then in possession of the Irish. It was held by Captain Barnwell, with 120 men, who immediately surrendered, and the place was occupied by a detachment of English troops.

The loss of the siege guns delayed all offensive operations against the city for over a week. In the meantime the men were busily employed in constructing forts and excavating trenches. The English lines extended from Pennywell on the right, following the course of the heights in a horseshoe form, round by the back of the present Waterworks, and along the slight elevation now occupied by the Gaol and Roches-Street, the extreme left resting on the Shannon. Between this and the fortifications the sappers and miners were slowly working their way to the walls. By the 17th the trenches were occupied by seven regiments and the redoubt in front of the citadel fell into the hands of the English. The place was of no use, for it was commanded by the walls, and a new Irish fort near the counterscarp[3] commanded the trenches and put a stop to further progress for a time. Some heavy guns arrived the same day from Waterford and were mounted on Ireton's fort.

On the night of the 18th, an attempt was made to surprise the Irish fort before mentioned, but failed, owing to the gallantry of the few who held it. The repulse was followed by a sortie from the garrison. The night was dark and the besiegers, ignorant of the ground, were thrown into confusion and could not tell friend from foe. Two parties, one of English and the other of Danes, kept up a fire upon one another for two hours without discovering their mistake. In the end the garrison retired into the city, having caused considerable damage, whilst suffering scarcely any loss themselves.

On the 20th it was determined that the fort must be taken at all hazards. All that day a battery of three pieces had been playing on it at a distance of only 150 yards, and the walls were greatly injured. At two o'clock in the afternoon the assault was ordered. A hundred and twenty grenadiers rushed from the trenches under a heavy musketry fire and succeeded in planting a ladder against the wall. Colonel Belcastle was first up, and into the fort, followed by the grenadiers. A fierce hand to hand struggle took place in the narrow confines within, and sixty of the defenders were slain. The grenadiers also suffered severely, but were continually reinforced by parties from the trenches, though they were exposed to a vigorous fire from the defenders. For several hours the conflict was maintained and even threatened at times to become a general engagement. In order to clear the walls, two batteries of eight guns each swept the fortifications, and another, of twelve guns, kept throwing red hot shot into the city. In the midst of the terrible scene a large quantity of powder in an Irish battery ignited accidentally, and blew up with a great explosion killing many of the gunners and inflicting much loss. The garrison at length adopted more vigorous measures. A sally was made with two thousand horse and foot under the command of Colonel Luttrel at the hour of relieving guard in the trenches. The new regiments coming fresh to the front renewed the battle, which was long and obstinately contested. So well directed was the Irish musketry, that of a detached party of twenty, not one came off without a wound, and the commander, Captain Lacy, was shot through the head. Many of the English were falling, and at last William drew off his forces, having first succeeded in demolishing the obnoxious tower.

During this prolonged attack, the King exposed himself to every danger with his accustomed coolness and on one occasion had a very narrow escape. He was riding by Ireton's fort, and was about to enter a gap, when he was addressed by an officer who wished to speak with him. At that very instant a cannon shot, said to have been fired from a gun on the tower of St. Mary's, struck the spot towards which he was moving and so near that he was covered with dust.

By the evening of the 21st a new battery was completed almost under the walls and immediately opened fire so as to effect a breach. On the 25th all the English works were finished and an incessant cannonade was kept up on the part of the fortifications near St. John's

A painting of The Siege of Limerick, dedicated to the women of the city, by 19th-century artist K. MacManus.

Gate. Next day the trenches were advanced to within twenty paces of the ditch. A breach, twelve yards wide, was made in the walls and the palisades in the counterscarp were beaten down. The engineers assured the King that the breach was practicable and could not be further enlarged for want of cannon balls. It was resolved to take the city by mines, and orders were given to attack the covered way and the towers on each side of the breach as soon as possible.

Within the city every precaution was made for a conflict which it was well known must decide the fate of the campaign. The breach could not be repaired in time, but the space inside being clear of houses, an entrenchment was thrown up, and some light guns mounted whose fire swept the area and commanded the opening. On either side nothing was left undone which the military skill and science of the period could effect. The morrow would tell the result.

It was in the afternoon of the 27th of August that the grand assault was made on the breach. The storming party consisted of five hundred grenadiers, supported by ten thousand men. Exactly at half-past three everything was in readiness for the final effort. The troops took up their respective positions in silence. Three signal guns boomed from Ireton's fort. Scarcely had the reverberations ceased, when the grenadiers leaped from the trenches, fired their pieces, threw their grenades, and with loud shouts rushed towards the breach. Here a fierce hand to hand encounter took place. So impetuous was the attack of the grenadiers, that after a short and deadly struggle, the Irish troops fell back, the English succeeded to their place, and some of them pressed into the streets and lanes of the town. Those within became thus exposed to a cross fire from the entrenchments which checked their further progress. The second line of attack, under Count Solmes, had advanced to the counterscarp and then halted in accordance with their orders. A brief lull ensued, such as precedes the thunderstorm. The garrison, rallied by Sarsfield, recovered from their sudden surprise. They re-formed their broken ranks, drove their assailants before them out over the breach, and scarce one who entered survived to tell of his exploit. The walls were again in the possession of their defenders and the breach was held by firm and resolute men. Again the breach was assaulted, and the engagement renewed with great fury. More troops pressed up from the English lines, and on the other side reinforcements poured into the city from the Clare side and strengthened the garrison. From the fortifications a deadly hail was poured upon the advancing columns. The spirit of the defenders was now roused to desperation and the enthusiasm communicated itself to the civilians and even to the women. These heroines, emulating the example of their sisters of Derry, took active part in the struggle. Undismayed by the terrible sights and scenes amid which they moved, they tended the wounded, succoured the fallen, and carried ammunition to the walls. They stood within the deadly breach whose stones they hurled at their assailants. They even advanced in front of the Irish ranks, into the vacant space between the two contending armies, so that sometimes they were nearer the English regiments than they were to their own countrymen, and when all missiles failed, attacked them with their tongues.

During the thick of the fight a part of the Brandenburgh regiment got possession of the Black Battery. According to one set of authorities, the powder accidentally took fire, according to others, a mine had been prepared for this contingency, and now exploded under them. At all events the battery blew up destroying all within it and upon it. The Brandenburghers were nearly annihilated and the adjacent ground was strewed with fragments of human bodies.

Three attempts had now been made to storm the breach, and three times the advancing columns had been driven back with great loss. Late in the evening the last effort was made. Again the attacking regiments were drawn up under the eyes of King William and hurled against the defenders who never yielded an inch. Standing shoulder to shoulder they flung back their assailants, as a tall cliff repels the waves that dash against its massive front. William anxiously watched the result of his last movement. The courage and determination of the Irish extorted from him words of admiration, even though the repulse of his best troops shewed him that to continue the engagement would only entail still greater loss. He therefore stopped all further operations and recalled his broken battalions. The boom of the cannon, the rattle of the musketry, the shouts of the combatants ceased. The noise of the conflict died away in silence, and the light of the setting sun illumined the battered walls and smiled upon the gallant band who held them against the flower of the English army, led by the greatest captain of his time.

According to the official list, the English lost on this occasion five hundred killed and eleven hundred wounded; but other authorities put down the loss at a much higher figure. Next day the soldiers were anxious to renew the battle but William thought it prudent to raise the siege. The abundant rain that had lately fallen rendered the ground so soft that movement was difficult. The Shannon was rising in such a manner as to endanger the fords, the season was now late, and the ravages of disease were beginning to make themselves felt. The batteries were kept in operation a little time longer, but a storm of wind and rain on the 29th decided matters finally. The heavy guns were brought off with difficulty, and on the last day of August the camp was broken up and the army departed into Winter quarters. William proceeded to England, leaving the command, first to Count Solmes, then to General Ginkle.

CHAPTER VI

Siege by Ginkle—1691

IT WAS EARLY SUMMER in the year 1691 before the rival forces were ready to take the field again. The English were collected at Mullingar, splendidly equipped, and commanded by Ginkle having under him Tollemache and Mackay who had just reduced the Scottish Highlands. The Irish were poorly clad and very badly supplied with the necessaries of war, and to complete their misfortune, the more important commands were bestowed upon a number of French officers whom James had sent over. The chief of these was St. Ruth, and under him were d'Usson and d'Tessé, whom it is customary to describe as capable leaders and able generals. An empty title rewarded the heroism and devotion of Sarsfield.

The campaign opened with the siege of Ballymore Castle in Westmeath, the advanced post of the Irish, which surrendered. Here Ginkle was joined by the Duke of Wirtemburg and Count Nassau with a body of foreign mercenaries. At the head of an army of eighteen thousand men he now marched upon Athlone, which was rightly regarded by both sides as the key of the position. Colonel Grace, who had so successfully defended the town in the previous year, had been removed, and his place was filled by a Frenchman, d'Usson. St. Ruth's headquarters were three miles distant. Ginkle appeared before the place on the 19th of June. 'His master ought to hang him' remarked St. Ruth, 'for attempting to take the town, mine ought to hang me if I lose it.' The half of the town on the left bank of the river was easily taken, but that was of little consequence. The bridge which joined the two banks was broken down and the ford was almost impassable. At the end of the month Ginkle saw he must either succeed or retreat at once. Whilst St. Ruth was persuading Sarsfield that the ford could not be attempted, and contemptuously rejecting every suggestion of the Irish soldier, Mackay dashed across with two thousand men, and to his astonishment and anger St. Ruth saw the place taken under his very eyes. Amongst those who fell fighting gallantly at his post was the old grey-headed veteran, Colonel Grace.

St. Ruth fell back on Aughrim, thirty miles distant, where his troops occupied a rising ground defended in front by a deep bog. Thither Ginkle followed him and gave battle. St. Ruth showed his jealousy by ordering Sarsfield far to the rear, commanding him not to stir from the spot till ordered to do so. The result of the engagement was the total defeat of the Irish army, as on the death of St. Ruth by a cannon ball the only person capable of taking the command had been kept in ignorance of everything. The fall of Galway followed, its garrison being permitted to join the main body, as did also that of Sligo. All Ireland was now in possession of the English except the old city by the Shannon.

During the previous twelve months the citizens of Limerick had done all in their power to make good their losses. The fortifications had been strengthened. The breach was repaired. New works were erected on the site of the Black Battery. The walls received a lining of great thickness which rendered them bomb proof. Some supplies had been received from James which, though not in such quantities as had been expected, were yet sufficient for all necessary purposes. The Irish army lay on the right bank of the Shannon, the outposts on the other side being abandoned. The cavalry were encamped in Clare and the main body of the infantry were in Limerick. Here also were the Duke of Tyrconnell, Lord Lieutenant, and the chief officials of the Jacobite Government. D'Usson, who lost Athlone, was on the death of St. Ruth appointed Governor of Limerick and commander of the army.

Ginkle, taught by the events of the previous year, resolved to act with great caution. He re-crossed the Shannon at Banagher, and proceeding by way of Nenagh arrived on the 14th of August at Cahirconlish. On the same day Tyrconnell died of apoplexy, not without a dark suspicion of poison having been administered to him.

His remains were interred the following night in St. Mary's Cathedral, but the exact spot is unknown. The provisional government was nominally entrusted to Lords Justices, but the real authority remained with d'Usson.

On the second approach to Limerick care was taken that the siege artillery should this time be provided with a suitable escort and the train arrived in safety from Athlone. On the 15th, Ruvigni, with fifteen hundred horse and a thousand foot, under the command of the Prince of Hesse, together with six pieces of artillery, was ordered to inspect the city, the Commander-in-chief accompanying them over the well known ground. They advanced to within a short distance of the fortifications and viewed the place for a considerable time, noting carefully every change and every improvement.

On the 18th, Sir William King, who had previously been Governor of Limerick and had been detained in prison, effected his escape and arrived at the English camp.

The season was wet and delayed active operations for a short time, but the weather becoming more favourable it was considered advisable to advance. The squadron which lay in the Shannon was ordered to take a position nearer the city. Each regiment had already two thousand fascines[1] provided beforehand. The army was directed to advance without beat of drum, so as not to attract particular attention. There was an advanced guard of nine hundred horse and dragoons, supported by a thousand foot and two hundred grenadiers. These marched in two divisions at the head of each wing, with four field pieces and twenty-five pioneers. Then came the main body of the horse, each soldier carrying his fascine before him on the saddle. Next appeared the solid masses of the infantry, 'their ranks one blaze of scarlet'. The artillery and baggage were kept well in rear.

The advanced guard proceeded from Cahirconlish to a house where the road divided and then halted till the infantry came up. The army then divided into two columns, one taking the road to the right, the other that to the left. Each wing was disposed in order of battle, and both proceeded slowly and cautiously towards the city. The Irish opened a well directed fire which killed several, including Colonel

A view from 'Honan's Quay'.

Donep, a Dane, and seriously checked the advance. The field pieces were then ordered to the front and a brisk cannonade opened before which the Irish gradually fell back, and the evening of that day, the 25th of August, saw the English army occupying the position it had held the previous year.

Next day a large quantity of war material arrived in camp in addition to all that had been provided. On the 27th, a body of horse under the Prince of Hesse was sent against Castle-Connell, which surrendered after two days, the garrison of 250 men being marched into camp as prisoners of war. About the same time Carrig-o-Gunnell surrendered to General Sgavenmore. Both castles were shortly afterwards demolished by gunpowder.

In the meantime the trenches were opened and other preliminary operations pushed on with vigour. Guns were mounted on their old positions and fortifications erected on the line of hills. On the 13th the siege guns opened a brisk fire on the Irish town the houses of which were speedily in flames and the inhabitants compelled to seek refuge in the English town or on the King's Island where a hasty camp was formed. That night the garrison made a sally to destroy the works then being constructed between Cromwell Fort and the Great Battery, but without success.

The Great Battery, by far the most formidable military work erected in Ireland, was placed on the low ridge which runs towards Park. It was within three hundred yards of the English town from which it was separated by the Abbey river and the swampy ground along its banks. During its construction the workmen were exposed to a heavy fire both from the battery at Baal's Bridge and the fort on the Island, but on the 8th of September the guns were placed in position. In the centre were eight large mortars. To the left extended a line of ten field pieces for throwing red hot shot, and to the right a similar range of twenty-five guns, all of the heaviest metal. No such display of artillery had ever been seen in Ireland before. Besides this the city was encircled with a ring of forts bristling with cannon, and all directed towards the devoted walls.

On the 8th of September a terrific fire was opened all along the line, and was returned by the besieged to the best of their ability, but the guns were not as powerful as those of the English. The Great Battery quickly made a considerable breach in the walls of the English town, near where the Dominican Abbey stood. The red hot shot told with great effect. The houses in many places were in flames which were with difficulty extinguished. Next day again the cannonading was kept up on the breach, which was considerably widened. It was debated by the generals whether an assault should be made on the breach, and preparations were going on for constructing a temporary bridge over this part of the Shannon. The universal opinion appeared to be that, even if the bridge were completed and a landing effected on the King's Island, yet the attacking force would be exposed to a destructive fire from the lines connecting the Great Irish Fort with the walls, which were manned by picked troops. Entrenchments had also been constructed within the breach itself, and from the results of a similar attack the previous year it was decided that the enterprise might probably be attended with disastrous consequences. The consideration of this matter was brought to a definite conclusion by the Irish secretly sending over a few daring men who burned the materials which had been collected for the bridge.

On the 12th the chief fire was directed on the Cathedral tower where a gun had been placed. The gun was dismounted and the gunner killed, but not before several English lives were lost. The cannon were then turned away from the Cathedral.

The prolonged resistance of the garrison – the strength of the fortifications – the unceasing vigilance of Sarsfield and the near approach of Winter, now compelled the English generals to consider their position very carefully, for up to the present they had accomplished absolutely nothing. There were only two courses open to them, either to abandon the siege altogether or turn the siege into a Winter blockade in the hope of reducing the city by famine. The first would be a confession of failure and defeat, and the second was very unpopular with the entire army who preferred anything rather than a winter in the trenches. As a last resource Ginkle determined to try what fortune might have in store for him on the Clare side. He

The Dominican Chapel.

constructed a battery at the most northern part of Corbally, to command the Parteen road. On the 15th of September he pretended to raise the siege and drew off some of his guns from the batteries, on which occasion Lord Lisburn was killed by a cannon shot. That night an advanced guard of four hundred grenadiers, with six hundred workmen, proceeded to the river under cover of darkness. By midnight they commenced the erection of a pontoon bridge which was thrown across to a little island called Illainarone and completed before day break. The morning was dark and foggy and the grenadiers and dragoons passed over unperceived. A strong body of horse and foot had been posted here under Colonel Clifford, but they were surprised and driven towards the city. A feeble attempt at resistance was made by some dismounted cavalry but they were dispersed by a charge of dragoons. The cavalry fled to the shelter of a wood, from whence they retreated to Limerick, but admittance being denied them they returned and having secured their tents and cattle retired to Six Mile Bridge, being joined by the remainder of the Irish horse.

Within the city the intelligence of the crossing excited the utmost consternation. Clifford was taken and imprisoned in the castle. An attempt was made to break down Quinpool Bridge, on the causeway to Thomond Bridge, but it did not succeed. The Lords Justices with their records and treasure barely escaped falling into the hands of the detachment sent forward to see what the Irish were doing. Ginkle being now within a mile of the city thought it prudent to issue a proclamation in the name of William and Mary, offering to all who should submit within eight days a free pardon, the restoration of their forfeited estates, and other benefits previously offered by the Lords Justices. Some were disposed to accept these terms, but the majority, relying on the long promised succour from France, considered the overtures unsatisfactory and rejected them.

Seeing that there was no hope of effecting a peaceable settlement and having received a large quantity of military stores, Ginkle resolved upon an attack in force. The pontoon bridge was removed from Illainarone to Carrig-a-Clouragh, where the army crossed the year before. Mackay and Talmash were left in command at Singland,

and a system of signals was arranged between them. The general himself, accompanied by Sgavenmore, Ruvigni, and the Prince of Wirtemburg, with almost all the horse, ten regiments of foot and fourteen pieces of artillery, moved to the river early on the morning of the 22nd. By noon the whole force had been transported across in safety and marched on the city. The advanced guard were repulsed at first by the Irish but more reinforcements coming rapidly up the Irish were compelled to give way before the superior numbers of the enemy. The English, fearing an ambuscade, advanced slowly and cautiously being careful to secure their line of march from all chance of surprise or disaster. It was not till four in the evening that the column came in front of Thomond Bridge. The Clare side of the bridge was protected by two forts, one at each corner, but the strongest defence was a line of gravel pits and quarries a little distance off, which was then held by eight hundred picked men. Ginkle having carefully reconnoitered the position, ordered a body of grenadiers forward to drive out the defenders. The grenadiers, under a heavy and deadly fire, rushed onward with their accustomed dash, and such was the impetuosity of the attack that the Irish gave way, though disputing every inch of the ground. A reinforcement under the command of Lacy arrived from the garrison to support them, and the conflict was renewed with great fury. The Irish charged their opponents again and again but were able to make no impression on the masses of the English and were compelled to fall back, borne down by the mere force of numbers, but retreating in good order under the shelter of King John's Castle. The outworks were gradually evacuated and fell into the hands of the English. Thomond Bridge became filled with the remains of the gallant band who for hours had checked the advance of an entire army. It was towards nightfall. So close and desperate had been the conflict that even in retreat and upon Thomond Bridge the fighting was still maintained hand to hand and English and Irish were mingled in confusion. A French officer commanded at the castle end of the bridge, and fearing lest the grenadiers might enter the city in the confusion, ordered the drawbridge to be raised, leaving the Irish troops to their fate. The drawbridge was raised. Into the yawning gulf were pushed headlong by their companions behind no less than one hundred and fifty men, who were swept away by the surging tide beneath. Six hundred more were cooped up on the narrow bridge and in the works at its further extremity, and so closely wedged together as to be unable to defend themselves from the fury of their pursuers. Quarter was neither given nor asked. The bridge was piled with dead, till the corpses rose higher than the battlements. Eight hundred Irish were sacrificed to secure the safety of King James's Frenchman.

This terrible slaughter and the horrible circumstances under which it took place destroyed all confidence in James's foreign allies. The spirit of the garrison was broken, and throughout the whole city were manifested indignation and disgust at the atrocious conduct of the French officer and the faithless nation to which he belonged. On the evening of the next day Sarsfield and Wauchop, a brave Scotchman, repaired to the English camp to seek a cessation of hostilities. A truce for three days was arranged and the prisoners on both sides were exchanged.

Negotiations for a permanent peace were entered upon with every desire on both sides to bring the siege to a termination. On the evening of the 27th Sarsfield and Wauchop dined with Ginkle and the chief officers of the English army and preliminaries were discussed. The Irish demanded an indemnity for past offences; that all Irish Roman Catholics should be restored to their estates which had been forfeited; that liberty of worship be granted to them; that perfect equality should exist between them and their Protestant fellow subjects; and that the Irish troops be placed on the same level as the rest of the royal forces, in case they were willing to serve against the enemies of England. These propositions were rejected by Ginkle as being inconsistent with the laws of England and exceeding his power to grant. Negotiations were accordingly broken off and orders were issued for prosecuting the siege. The garrison then requested to know what terms the General was empowered to grant and the conferences were resumed. On the 28th the officers of both armies met together and articles were mutually agreed upon, which Sir Theobald Butler was directed to reduce to writing. Sir Theobald is said to have made the articles more favourable than had been arranged, and this being detected in the draft some unpleasantness arose, points were finally adjusted. It was conceded that all Irish Roman Catholics should enjoy such privileges in the exercise of their religion as they possessed in the reign of Charles II, and it was promised that their majesties would endeavour to procure such further security as would preserve them from any further disturbance on this head. All included in the capitulation should enjoy their estates, such as they were legally entitled to in the reign of Charles II, and might pursue their several callings and professions freely. Noblemen and gentry were allowed to carry and use arms. The oath to be administered to all Roman Catholics who chose to submit was the oath of allegiance and no other. It was also agreed that all who wished to retire from the kingdom with their families and property and all soldiers who preferred foreign service should be conveyed to the continent at the expense of the government.

Whilst the treaty was being framed the soldiers of the two armies were on the most friendly terms and visited one anothers' quarters. The officers of the garrison were entertained in a series of dinner parties by the English generals. On the 3rd of October the famous treaty of Limerick was signed, most probably in the tent of the Duke of Wirtemburg, with whom the principal officers of both armies dined that evening, and most likely about sunset, as the formal occupation of the city under Tollemache was deferred till next day. The treaty consisted of two parts. The first related to the surrender of the city and was signed by the generals on both sides, the garrison being allowed to march out with all the honours of war. The second enumerated the conditions granted to the Irish nation and was signed by Ginkle and the Lords Justices. A clause in the latter which was omitted by the transcriber was inserted afterwards by William, who detected the omission, in his own handwriting. To the lasting disgrace of the English House of Commons the treaty was deliberately violated, though ratified by William and Mary. An act professing to confirm the articles was subsequently passed, but every stipulation of importance was carefully omitted. A few days after the signing of the treaty a French fleet arrived for the relief of the city.

The Treaty Stone, on which according to tradition the treaty was signed.

The capitulation being completed both Ginkle and Sarsfield endeavoured to secure the Irish regiments for their respective masters. The former sent an experienced officer to point out the great advantages possessed by the English service over that of a foreign monarch who had been but lukewarm in the cause of Ireland. Sarsfield and the clergy strongly urged the soldiers in favour of France, adding that they might soon be able to renew the conflict under more favourable circumstances.

On the morning of the 6th of October the Irish army, to the number of fourteen thousand men, assembled on the Clare side of the river. About three thousand, including the Ulster Irish, either withdrew to their homes or joined the English army. By far the larger number volunteered for foreign service, and in accordance with the treaty were conveyed to France, where they formed the nucleus of the famous Irish Brigades, whose valour was conspicuous on every battle field in Europe, and whose leaders were high in the confidence of princes. The noble Sarsfield died shortly afterwards, meeting a soldier's death on the field of Landen as he and his dragoons were victorious in the midst of a routed army. Nor in his dying moments was his country absent from his thoughts, for looking at the blood which flowed freely from his wounds he exclaimed – 'Oh that it had been for Ireland!'

The defeats of the Irish army during the campaigns of 1690 and 1691 are not to be attributed to any want of valour in the soldiers. What they could do when left to their own commanders was shown in the first siege of Limerick, and afterwards on many a hard fought continental battlefield. But no troops could succeed under such leaders as were forced upon the Irish. At the Boyne King James fled before the battle was lost. The neglect of d'Usson and the absurd self confidence of St. Ruth lost Athlone, whilst the latter's ridiculous vanity, united to his childish jealousy of the brilliant Sarsfield, caused the defeat and subsequent slaughter at Aughrim. The conduct of the nameless French officer at Thomond Bridge is beyond comment. The wonder is that the Irish troops under such commanders were able to make the stand they did, and that in spite of everything they still remained faithful to such a contemptible creature as the Stuart King.

CHAPTER VII

Old Limerick

THE ANCIENT CITY WHOSE HISTORY has been briefly recorded in the preceding pages was a very different place from the Limerick of today.[1] By far the larger portion of the present city had then no existence, nor was it called into being till very many years had passed away. The historic portion was then strictly limited to those parts called respectively the English town and Irish town. The English town situated at the western extremity of the King's Island, was the centre of the civil, military and ecclesiastical organisation. It was connected at an early period with the Clare side of the river by Thomond Bridge, and with the Limerick bank by Baal's Bridge. A wall pierced with numerous gates and fortified with strong towers surrounded the whole area. Of these walls some considerable portions still remain. They may be traced from Thomond Bridge by the graveyard of St. Munchin towards Watergate, when they turn sharply eastward, and may still be observed at the back of the Convent of Mercy, running nearly parallel to Island Road. Thence they continued to Baal's Bridge, but this portion has entirely disappeared. From Baal's Bridge they extended along the present George's Quay to the Potato Market, which occupies the site of the ancient harbour, the mouth of which was defended by batteries. The chief stronghold of the English town was King John's Castle, so called from the Monarch who ordered its erection. Even after the lapse of nearly seven centuries the castle is an imposing structure and one of the finest specimens of Norman military architecture to be found in the kingdom. The river front about two hundred feet in length is flanked by two massive round towers, each fifty feet in diameter, with walls ten feet thick. That near the

Eastgate sculp!

KING JOHN'S CASTLE, *at* LIMERICK.

bridge is considered to be the more ancient and bears on its front the marks of severe cannonading. The original entrance now disused is remarkably narrow, and lies between two tall and very strong round towers, whose appearance is most striking and imposing. Another tower of similar construction defended the corner where the walls took a course parallel to the river. The modern entrance is in Nicholas Street. At the angle towards the town there formerly stood a low square tower or platform capable of mounting five or six cannon, and in the lower storey was the sally port of the fortress. The square tower has long since been demolished, but a considerable extent of the wall connecting it with the tower by the river's edge has been preserved. The whole structure was surrounded by a deep broad moat supplied with water from the Shannon. Within the circuit of the walls a modern military barrack contrasting strangely with an ancient and venerable pile was erected in 1751. The castle was committed to the custody of a Constable. The last who held the post was Lord Gort, on whose death in 1840 the office ceased to exist. Near the castle stands St. Munchin's Church, which occupies the site of an ancient cathedral of Limerick. The original edifice is attributed to St. Munchin, or Manchin, in the middle of the 7th century, and is said to have been restored by the Danes during the time they held Limerick in their possession. The present Thomond Bridge is similar to that erected by King John with the exception of the drawbridge which was formerly at the city end. The old guard-house has long ago been demolished. A range of ancient houses opposite the castle, in one of which the Duke of Tyrconnell, Lord Lieutenant of Ireland under King James, breathed his last in 1691, has also disappeared.

Ancient Limerick was remarkable for the number, extent, and grandeur of its ecclesiastical edifices. The most imposing of these was the Dominican Convent. Two lofty ivy-covered walls and an interesting doorway within the grounds of the present Convent of Mercy are all that remain of this once famous establishment. The Abbey was founded in the early part of the 13th century by Donogh Cairbreagh O'Brien. Within its precincts were laid the bones of its founder, and many other Chieftains chose this as their final resting place. At

George Street, now O'Connell Street, Limerick.

various times no less than six bishops were interred in this spot, and here in 1345, John O'Grady, Archbishop of Cashel, was placed in his last home. In 1462, James, Earl of Desmond, a munificent contributor, was laid in a tomb worthy of its tenant. The Abbey had the honour of being erected into a university or place of general study in 1644. Prior to the suppression of the religious establishments by Henry VIII the Dominican Abbey possessed considerable wealth. The community owned the celebrated Lax Weir, St. Thomas's Island, Monabraher or the Friar's Bog on the Clare shore, as well as large territories in the neighbourhood. On the dissolution of the monasteries the edifice was allowed to fall into decay, and the lands were granted to the Earl of Desmond, and on his forfeiture to the Earl of Thomond. The Lax Weir was granted to the Corporation of Limerick in 1583. In the reign of Charles II a huge military barrack capable of holding eight hundred men, was erected in the grounds of the monastery, and doubtless served to complete the destruction of the sacred buildings.

The first regular religious community established in Limerick was that of the Canons of St. Augustine. According to Ware the Priory was founded in 1227 by Simon Minor, a citizen of Limerick. This establishment was situated near Baal's Bridge, between it and the Mall, but not a trace of it now remains. The head of this house had the first vote in the election of the Mayor and occupied a seat in the court next to the Mayor. At the time of the suppression the property of the Convent was granted to Edmond Sexton, in the hands of whose descendants it has since remained. Near the site of this building it may be remembered an Irish battery was erected which annoyed William's army on their march through Park. The Hermits of St. Augustine possessed an establishment in Quay Lane, on the site of the old City Courthouse. Some traces of the building may be observed exactly opposite the principal entrance to the Cathedral grounds. The nuns of the same order had a religious house founded by King Donald O'Brien in 1171 and dedicated to St. Peter. The place is still called St. Peter's Cell. It was situated near the town wall at the lower end of Pump Lane. At the suppression it was granted to Lord Milton and in the 18th century the Chapel was used by the Presbyterians as a place of worship up to the year 1776. A dwelling house was afterwards built on the site.

There was yet another famous Abbey, the Franciscan, founded in the 13th century by William de Burgho, son-in-law of Donald O'Brien. It stood just without the city walls, and occupied the greater part of the space between Sir Harry's Mall and Athlunkard Street, which part is still called St. Francis's Abbey. Traces of the buildings connected with this great Abbey may still be detected in the neighbourhood, but they are becoming fewer and fewer every day. Moroney, who visited Limerick in 1615, describes the buildings, as still standing but likely to fall.

Amid all the decay and destruction one memorable edifice still survives, having both escaped the hands of the destroyer and resisted the ravages of time. For close on seven centuries the lofty tower of St. Mary's Cathedral has looked down upon the busy life of the old fortress city crowded around its base. St. Mary's Cathedral was founded by the great Donald O'Brien, King of Limerick, about the time of the landing of the Normans. It is built upon the site of one of Donald's palaces which he gave up for the purpose. The entrance is so peculiar in ecclesiastical architecture, that of a pillared arch under the lofty tower in the middle of the west facade, as to lead some authorities to believe that this portion of the structure formed part of the original palace. The Cathedral was not originally as large as it is at present, many additions having been made from time to time. It was a basilica, consisting of nave, side aisles, transepts, and chancel, terminating not in a semi-circle but in a straight wall. In the 15th century very important changes were made. The round arch wherever possible had to give way to the pointed, chapels were added not harmonising in style with the ancient building, but widening the aisles and raising the interior walls.

The tower is 120 feet high. The upper portion is somewhat modern and replaced that injured during the sieges of 1690 and 1691. The Cathedral contains many ancient monuments. The most interesting is the lid of King Donald's stone coffin, which lies on the floor of one of the chapels. Here also may be found the altar stone removed from the east end. A monument to Richard Bultingford and Geoffrey

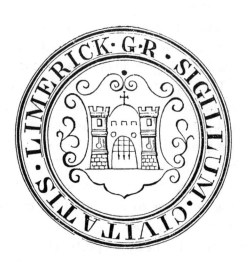

Top: Part of the coat of arms of Great Britain, which was used as the Mayor's Seal in 1768. Centre: Seal of Dean and Chapter of the Cathedral Church of the Blessed Virgin Mary, Limerick. Bottom: City Seal bearing the Limerick coat of arms used in the period 1714-30.

Galwey bears the date 1414. In the south wall of the chancel may be observed a black marble slab commemorating Bishop O'Dea, a munificent benefactor, who died in 1434. In the north transept are found two inscriptions, one in memory of John Ffox, Dean, and Geoffrey Arthur, Treasurer of the Cathedral, who died in 1519. A huge memorial in the north wall of the chancel was erected in memory of Donogh O'Brien, Earl of Thomond and Lord President of Munster. Having been injured by the soldiers of Ireton this monument was re-edified in 1678 as the inscription records. The two broken and defaced effigies reposing in one of the compartments are evidence of their vandalism. The Earl of Inchiquin (Murrough of the Burnings) was interred in the Cathedral with military honours in 1674, and Richard Talbot, Duke of Tyrconnell, in 1691, but no memorial marks the graves of either, nor is their position known.[2]

The Cathedral stood in the midst of, and was surrounded by, groups of ecclesiastical buildings which have been swept away. These were connected with the central pile by underground passages. On the north side of Bow Lane stood the college for minor canons, erected in the 13th century by Hubert de Burgh, Bishop of Limerick, who was consecrated in 1221. The massively built walls are still standing though greatly shattered. Two round arched doorways still remain and a curiously constructed window is preserved by being built up. The small grated window used as a lookout for the porter may be observed. The buildings in this quarter were also connected with the Cathedral by a house which spanned the lane, then much narrower than it is at present. The pathway has since been made considerably lower, as it now exposes the foundations of the minor canon's college. Between the college and the castle formerly stood St. Nicholas's Abbey, which was destroyed during the siege of 1691, but some traces of it may yet be observed. The ancient episcopal palace was situated near St. Munchin's Church, but the site has long been occupied by small cottages.

The streets of the English town, with the single exception of the Main Street or St. Nicholas Street, were very narrow and crooked, and could only be traversed by foot passengers. On each side rose tall and lofty houses now crumbling into decay. In some places they have tumbled down, leaving empty spaces which have not been built upon. These old houses with their quaint curved gables turned towards the street, give certain portions of the English town a peculiarly foreign look. Some few years ago Mary Street might almost be mistaken for a piece of some old continental city, but the resemblance is now almost obliterated. The existing brick houses have been built upon the foundations of still older structures, whose materials have been liberally utilized by the modern builder. The fall of the more recent portions often brings to light and exposes to view some relics and traces of the earlier occupant of the site. Whittamore's Castle, between Mary Street and the river, is a striking example of the old fortified residences, strongly built of cut limestone and apparently constructed so as to stand a siege. The wall towards the river is still standing almost entire and the doors and windows are in very good preservation. It is popularly called the Castle of Limerick and also Sarsfield's Castle, from a tradition that it was occupied by that distinguished general during the last two sieges. At the head of Creagh Lane the demolition of some houses has brought to light a beautiful chimney piece still standing in a gable. In Athlunkard Street are the remains of a castle, one of the walls of which has been utilized in the erection of a drinking fountain. The formation of the street necessarily led to the destruction of the remainder of the castle. The most remarkable of the private residences which have lasted down to the present day is without doubt that at the corner of Nicholas Street, near where the Exchange stood till quite recently. It is said to have been so far back as 1600 the residence of Sir Geoffrey Galway, Mayor of Limerick in that year, and tradition points it out as the house in which Ireton died of the plague in 1651.[3] Subsequently it was known as the Gridiron Hotel, but is now let in tenements and rapidly falling into decay. The lower story is of high antiquity and the not improbable conjecture has been hazarded that here we have existing before us the remains of the Kings of Limerick, which we know once stood on the spot.

The Irish town situated on the Limerick side of the Shannon is more modern than that portion just described, of which it was originally no

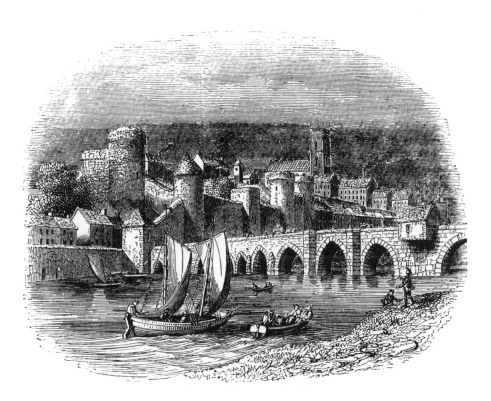

A portion of the old walls of Limerick town.

more than a suburb. It was not till the 14th century that the walls were begun, and St. John's Gate was not completed till 1495. Baal's Bridge formed the connecting link between the two parts of the city. The origin of the name is somewhat obscure. By some it is associated with a heathen Prince called Baal, who is considered to have erected the first structure. The name in Irish means Bald Bridge, that is, 'without battlements'. It is quartered upon the arms of the Galway family in commemoration of an ancestor of theirs, John de Burgho, commonly called John of Galway, who held the city in 1361 against an attacking force of the O'Brien's. Down to the period of the last siege Baal's Bridge supported two rows of houses upon it, thus leaving a very narrow passage between them. One of these rows was removed, but the other continued to stand as long as the old bridge remained, which was taken down in 1830, and the present structure occupies its site.

Of the old walls which surrounded the Irish town the eastern portion still remains in very fair preservation. The height in some parts is fully forty feet or more. The wall proper is backed by a rampart of earth about twenty feet in thickness. Trees were planted, many of which remain, and Ferrar states that this was a very fashionable promenade of the citizens in the 18th century. A small swivel gun and some iron cannon were discovered in the earthen mound and have been planted on the battlements. In the centre of this part of the wall was a sally port, the entrance to which is at the end of Father Quin's lane. A short flight of stone steps give access to the battlements. On the outer face of the wall may be observed traces of masonry which show that this portion was strengthened by an external tower, probably that known as the Devil's Tower, which has been completely demolished. The present St. John's Hospital, formerly the Fever Hospital, identifies and preserves some most interesting remains of the old fortifications. The western wing of the hospital was the ancient guardhouse of the citadel. The walls are of great thickness and the outer gate was defended with a portcullis, the groove in which it moved being easily discovered. Part of the ancient city wall is still attached and the entrance gate to the hospital was the town gate of the citadel. To the east of the hospital a considerable portion of the wall remains standing, at the end of which may be observed the stump of the famous Black Battery. This was the neighbourhood in which the fierce contest of 1690 took place. 'The masked battery was placed at what is now the extreme corner of Curry's lane, exactly opposite the breach.'[4] The breach which is twelve yards wide may be distinguished from the adjacent parts of the fortifications, by having been built up with clay instead of mortar. In the front wall of the hospital is a stone bearing the name of John Creagh, Mayor, with the date 1st May 1651. An old blackened and leafless pear tree in the yard of the hospital was till quite recently pointed out as having been in existence in the time of the sieges and as having supplied Sarsfield with fruit during that time. From the corner occupied by the Black Battery there may be obtained a fine view of the surrounding heights and of the ground occupied by the operations conducted during the last two sieges. This line of hills has from time immemorial been intimately connected with the history of the city. Here St. Patrick is said to have seen the vision of an angel, and his well and rocky 'bed' are still pointed out and held in reverence. Here he baptized Catha or Carthen, Chief of a neighbouring district. Many conflicts with the Danes, as previously stated, were waged on these heights during the centuries in which these foreign aggressors were endeavouring to push their conquests farther and farther inland. Here swept by the great northern army of invasion in 1088, which ravaged and burned the greater part of the country. They returned home to the North bringing with them the head of one of their leaders, O'Ruarc, sur-named the cock, who had fallen in battle a short time before and whose head was exposed to public view on 'the hillocks of Singland'.[5] During each of the three sieges the range of hills formed the chief centre of the attacking forces. They were occupied during Ireton's time, but the range was rather far for the cannon of the period and closer quarters had to be sought. In 1690 and 1691 the heights were a line of batteries from whence a storm of shot was poured against the walls and into the city. The site of the principal battery is now occupied by the reservoir of the Waterworks and a practised eye can detect the traces of others. From thence to the city walls extends a gently sloping space, through which the trenches were pushed, and near the centre exists a very slight elevation, which was occupied with an Irish redoubt. Some short distance from the city, by the side of one of the old roads, may be found a pillar of masonry about five feet in height, but formerly much higher, on which it is traditionally reported the Royal Standard of England was displayed in 1690. A well still called after King William may be found a little further off on the same road to the right, and the 'Camp Field' needs no explanation. The little river, Groody, a tributary of the Shannon, was a very important defence in former times, for its waters were not then confined between banks as they are now, but turned the adjacent fields into a morass.

The spots memorable for the principal crossings of the Shannon by William and Ginkle are sufficiently marked by the island of Illaina-rone, and the 'Chain Rock', near Kilquane churchyard, just above the millrace. On the opposite side a similar ledge of limestone is pointed out as having secured the southern end of the bridge of boats or pontoons. The diminutive castle in the middle of the Lax Weir is still in good repair and is quite a curiosity because of its size. To conclude our survey of the old city, the lines of the great entrenched camp constructed by Ireton in 1650 are yet discernible at the north east end of the King's Island. By a strange revolution of fortune the great fort during the two subsequent sieges formed one of the strongest positions of the Irish and protected the city from attack on that side.

The only trace now remaining of the Danish possession of Limerick is the name of the Lax Weir, from the Danish word 'lax', which means a salmon. This in itself is sufficient to show that the invaders took no permanent hold of the country and that they never conquered it or imposed a Sovereign or Monarch as they did in England.

CHAPTER VIII

The Growth of
Modern Limerick[1]

FOR SEVENTY YEARS after the last siege Limerick was regarded as a fortress. Sentries patrolled the ramparts, guards were posted at important points of the fortifications. The gates were locked at nightfall and kept locked all Sunday. It was not till 1760 that these precautions were considered unnecessary and that Limerick was declared to be no longer a fortress. The walls were dismantled and as if by magic a new and extensive city sprang into existence. As if the energy of the citizens had been accumulating all these years, the next decade witnessed a display of activity without a parallel in civic annals. During the seventy years before referred to, no improvements had been carried out except the erection of some street lamps and the building of a market house on the site of an old castle in the Irish town. But now a change took place. George's Quay was constructed and lined with excellent houses. The tower and guardhouse on Old Thomond Bridge were demolished. The houses on one side of Baal's Bridge were thrown down. A new bridge on the site of the present Mathew Bridge was commenced, and Cornwallis Street the forerunner of the handsome thoroughfares of the present city was called into existence. This was the work of one single year.

Then followed the erection of the Custom House, and in 1764 of the City Court House, Lock Quay was completed. Charlotte's Quay connected Baal's Bridge with the New Bridge and was speedily occupied with tall brick houses and ornamented shortly afterwards with the Assembly Rooms. Sir Harry's Mall followed in 1767 and in 1769 the Right Hon E.S. Pery mapped out the streets and squares

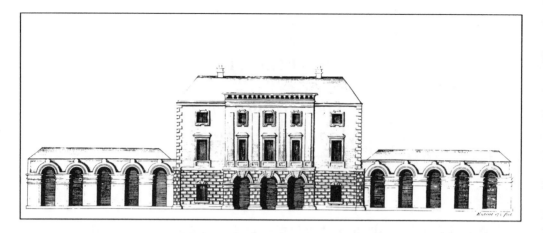

The Customs House.

*Wellesley Bridge took eleven years to build and was opened in 1835 by the
Earl of Mulgrave, Lord Lieutenant of Ireland.*

whose regularity is so striking a feature in the modern portion. Before the close of the 18th century these streets were the scene of busy life and of unexampled commercial activity.

In this expansion of enterprise the name of Mr Patrick Arthur, of a family long identified with Limerick, stands pre-eminent. He transformed the swampy banks of the Shannon into a noble quay, on which was speedily built a fine range of houses called to this day Arthur's Quay after their proprietor. Rutland Street, previously erected from the extremity of the New Bridge, was by him extended into Patrick Street. Other wealthy merchants followed Mr. Arthur's example. Lines of quays bordered the banks of the river and new streets were pushed out over the swamps where snipe found a refuge and over fields recently green with grass or yellow with the golden corn. The new residences were occupied by the merchants and traders whose places of business were in the other part of the town, but by little and little the private residences were pushed forward and onward by the advancing tide of human life, till today the scenes of busiest activity are in these portions of the city, which were swampy meadows only a hundred years ago. The history of every city tells the same tale, but in very few has the transformation been so rapid and so complete.

At the beginning of the 19th century the Corporation endeavoured to impose their authority upon the New Town as it was called. Their claims were resisted by a large body called the Independents, who desired self government and freedom from unjust taxation. After a long and stubborn resistance on the part of the Corporation, the New Town was placed under the control of a body called the Commissioners of St. Michael's Parish. They continued to exercise authority till their powers merged into the Reformed Municipal Corporation.

In 1805 the merchants of Limerick erected the Commercial Buildings, now the Town Hall, in Rutland Street, as a place of meeting. Ten years afterwards they were incorporated by royal charter into the Chamber of Commerce of Limerick. Later on the body removed from the Commercial Buildings to a more central situation in George Street.

The year 1808 saw the foundation of the County Courthouse, which was ready for the transaction of business in the summer of 1810. It is a quadrangular building of hewn limestone with a Doric portico of four massive columns. The architects, Messrs Nicholas & William Hannon, were natives of the county. A Theatre was erected in George Street, which not proving a success was purchased by the Augustinian Order and converted into a church. In the next year the City Gaol replaced the old edifice in Mary Street, which had fallen into decay. It stands on the site of the old Deanery House and garden. The County Gaol, near the Cork road, was begun in 1817 and completed in 1821, at a cost of £23,000. A tower built of hewn stone forms the centre of the whole. Five ranges of buildings extend from the tower in which are the cells. The whole is surrounded by a wall twenty feet in height, and two and a half thick, and outside the entrance of the Gaol is a lofty iron palisading. On the opposite side of the road is the County Hospital, opened for the reception of patients in 1811. In the same neighbourhood is the Lunatic Asylum, which was completed in 1826 at a cost of £30,000. It is constructed of limestone, lined with brick. The centre is an octagon from which four wings diverge. Under the present Medical Superintendent (Dr Courtnay), many important improvements have been effected, and the Limerick Lunatic Asylum is regarded as one of the best managed institutions of the kind in the empire.[2]

Barrington's Hospital was founded by Sir Joseph Barrington and his sons in 1831 at a cost of £10,000. All donors of £20 and annual subscribers of three guineas are governors. The governors elect the committee of management each year. The hospital has not received the amount of support it deserves. Though the Corporation have lately given a grant, the funds of this most deserving institution are lamentably deficient. Up to a short time ago a *Mont de Piete*[3], established in 1837, stood close by. The building was a long time disused and had fallen into decay. The cupola and pillars formed a peculiar object indeed, till the whole was demolished in 1884.

In addition to the ancient Baal's Bridge and Thomond Bridge, which had existed for centuries, it was felt that the outlets of the city required to be improved. Communication was opened up in 1824 between Park Bridge and the New Bridge by the construction of

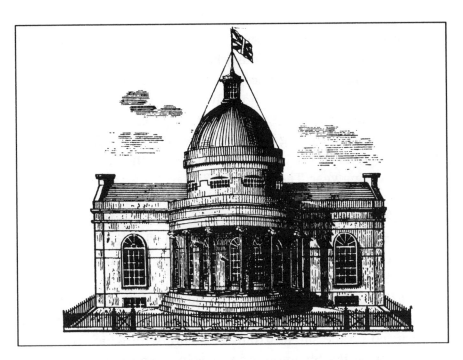

Monte de Piete, a charitable pawn office, founded by Matthew Barrington and opened in 1837.

Athlunkard Street. At the same time, that portion known as St. Francis's Abbey, which previously belonged to the county, was now attached to the city and placed under control of the magistrates. Communication with Clare and Galway was opened up by the erection of Athlunkard Bridge, in 1830, at a cost of £7,000. Tolls were required from all crossing it till 1884, when they were abolished. Old Baal's Bridge was taken down and replaced by the present structure in the following year. The Wellesley Bridge Act was passed in 1823. The bridge took eleven years to build and the Commissioners spent nearly £90,000 on its construction. It was opened in 1835 by the Earl of Mulgrave, Lord Lieutenant of Ireland. The bridge was not freed from toll till 1883, on which occasion the Corporation changed the name to Sarsfield Bridge.

In 1826 a Company was formed for supplying the city water, laid down into their houses by means of pipes. A large reservoir was constructed on the site of Cromwell's Fort, with which water was pumped from the Shannon, from a point a considerable distance above the town. A second reservoir has been subsequently erected on the Ennis road.

The old Theatre in Cornwallis Street was replaced in 1841 by the Theatre in Henry Street, which was erected by Mr Joseph Fogerty, and now that the Dublin Royal is destroyed, is probably the largest Theatre in Ireland. In the same year the Union Workhouse was opened for the reception of paupers, and the Jurisdiction of the Recorder was transferred to the Chairman of Quarter Sessions. The New Town had been lighted with gas since 1824, and the energy and enterprise of the citizens was rapidly raising Limerick to the important position it has since occupied.

In the early years of the 19th century Limerick possessed a curiosity which was without a parallel in the empire. Roche's Hanging Gardens which have now disappeared were long a source of interest to strangers visiting the city. The following description of them is from Fitzgerald's *History*.

In 1808 William Roche, Esq., being much occupied with the care of an extensive banking concern, devised a plan for his personal recreation to

Mr Roche's Garden, Limerick.

Published by Geo. M Kern. — Limerick.

Mr Roche's Hanging Gardens.

obviate the necessity of occasional absence from his residence. He accordingly took some ground at the rere of his house in George-street, and having raised a number of arches, converted the interior of them into stores for holding wine, spirits, and other goods. The height of the arches is various, the top of the two side ones being nearly forty feet from the street, and that of the middle arches twenty-five. On these he formed elevated terraces, the highest of which is ornamented with forcing or hot houses, heated by glass and flues. Some of these produce grapes, pineapples, peaches, etc., others are orangeries and conservatories, and the hothouses are united in the angles by globular greenhouses. The middle terraces is [sic] devoted to vegetables and hardy fruit trees; the lower to flowers of every form, scent, and hue. A vacant space in the garden also raised on arches is appropriated to forcing melons, cucumbers, etc. Flights of steps lead from one elevation to another, and the whole occupies more than an English acre of ground; the side terraces are one hundred and fifty feet long by thirty wide; the central terrace one hundred and eighty feet long by forty wide; and the lower two hundred feet long and one hundred feet wide, exclusive of the melon or cucumber ground, which is about eighty feet square. The facade of this building extends opposite the houses of the Earl of Limerick and the Bishop about two hundred feet. The top of the highest wall is seventy feet above the adjacent street and commands a most extensive prospect of the city and the windings of the Shannon, with the gentlemen's villas on either shore to a considerable distance. The depth of earth on the gardens averages about five feet, and the stores underneath are protected from the penetration of moisture by flags cemented together and by channels of lead, which convey the redundant moisture through perpendicular tubes of the same metal concealed in the abutments of the arches and thence by horizontal sewers to the main sewer of the street. In dry weather by stopping the communication with the perpendicular tubes the water is retained and repelled into the different channels under the garden surface. The rain water which falls on the glass sashes is also retained in cisterns on the forcing houses, and manure is brought up by mechanical means, which renders the labour less than if the garden were on the natural surface. The whole expense of this singular structure was £15,000; but Mr Roche's speculation respecting the stores proved to be well founded, for the Government took them at a fine of £10,000 and a rent of £300 a year.

A little more than a hundred years ago there was no public mode of conveyance between Limerick and any other city in Ireland. Travellers generally proceeded in small companies and on horseback, but very few went any distance from home except in case of necessity.

The first attempt to open up a regular means of communication with the Capital was made in 1760 – that year of wonderful progress. A weekly coach was established, which accomplished the journey to Dublin in four days. The same distance can now be done in less than the number of hours. The old route was from St. John's Square over Baal's Bridge, Thomond Bridge, and thence by Killaloe. After an experience of twenty years the coach was improved and the route changed to Clare Street, and thence on to Nenagh, by which the time was reduced to two days. In 1815 Mr Bianconi established a line of communication between Clonmel and Limerick, one of the very first with which his name is connected, and from that time onward a network of coach routes connected all the important towns of Ireland till an improved means of locomotion rendered them no longer necessary. In 1848 the first line of railway was opened, connecting Limerick with Tipperary, which was extended to Waterford in 1854. This provided an easy mode of access to Dublin and Cork. The line to Castle-Connell was opened in 1858, that to Foynes and Ennis in the subsequent year. The Cork Direct was opened in 1862 and the Rath-keale and Newcastle in 1865. The latter has been extended to Listowel, so that the journey to Tralee, which by the old coach route lasted 11½ hours can now be comfortably made in 3½ hours.

The splendid line of quays from the Wellesley Bridge, finished in 1848, was supplemented in 1853 by the floating dock which encloses a water space of about eight acres, and is capable of accommodating eighty vessels. The electric light was added in 1880 and a public clock erected near the lock gates. Near the docks is the immense corn store belonging to Messrs J. Bannatyne and Sons, which replaces one burned down in 1878. This store has five lofts, each capable of holding a ship's cargo, and is provided with several grain elevators. The Corkanree embankment has enclosed a considerable area and forms an agreeable promenade. A square tower has been erected at the extremity by the citizens to commemorate the 'probity and energy' of Mr William Spillane, during whose mayoralty in 1870 the embankment was completed.

The year which witnessed the opening of the docks also saw the establishment of the Great Munster Fairs, which have a world wide reputation. The number has been lately increased from two to four in the year but this is considered a doubtful advantage.

The Harbour Commissioners have improved the navigation of the river by removing obstructions, clearing away rocks and shoals, placing buoys and lights at important points, and otherwise rendering access to the city easy and safe. The prosperity of Limerick has been carefully advanced by the association of merchants who form the Chamber of Commerce, the formation of which has been already referred to. This body has bestowed its attention upon each department of trade and opened up facilities for its successful cultivation. They undertook the management of the butter trade, encouraged the linen trade, contributed large sums to alleviate the sufferings of the operatives in times of depression or distress, and in fine, much of the improvement of the city is due to the early enterprise and public spirit of that body. The efficiency of the Chamber of Commerce in recent years has been fully maintained by its present President, Sir James Spaight, the late Secretary, Mr William Carroll, and present Secretary, Mr M. O'Gorman. The building is in George Street, and contains a commodious reading room and library. There are also to be found here several pictures of civic interest, such as the election of Mr T. Spring Rice for the city in 1820, a full length portrait of the same gentleman, executed by Sir M.A. Shee, P.R.A., a view of the Abbey River in 1816, old St. John's Square and the entry of George IV into Dublin.

The well known firm of Messrs J.N. Russell and Sons has long been identified with the establishment and extension of the corn and flour trade. The name is not of recent introduction for we find a J. Russell filling the office of Mayor so far back as 1216, and it occasionally reappears at intervals ever since. The flour mills of the Messrs Russell were amongst the largest and most extensive in Ireland, and their coasting vessels were known in every port and harbour in the kingdom. In 1827 they introduced the use of steam into their mills at Newtown Pery, and ten years later the stores in Henry Street were erected owing to the large increase of business consequent on the change. The same firm established mills at Lock, Corbally, Plassy, Garryowen and Askeaton, many of which unfortunately are now idle. They also erected the great factory at Lansdowne for flax spinning and weaving, the success of which did not justify the immense sum expended upon its construction. Messrs James Bannatyne & Sons at present occupy the foremost position in this branch of commercial development. Their celebrated mills at Roche Street have recently been fitted up with the most improved modern machinery, and the result is the production of a class of flour which defies competition both in quality and price. The Mount-Kennet mills, formerly the property of the Messrs Harris, are also in full operation under the same firm.

The bacon trade of Limerick has made the name of the city pre-eminent in that department all over the world. The trade always flourished, but in 1826 it received a most important impetus from Mr John Russell, an English gentleman, whose establishment became the largest in Ireland. Since then the trade has been enormously successful, Matterson's hams and Shaw's breakfast bacon being quite unrivalled. The establishments of the Messrs Matterson, Shaw and Denny, are well worth a visit. By these three firms about ten thousand pigs are slaughtered weekly. The Messrs Shaw were the first to introduce electric lighting on a large scale in Limerick, and their example was rapidly followed by other firms. In spite of keen foreign competition the Limerick bacon maintains its supremacy as being the best article of the kind in the market, all other competitors for public favour being a long way behind.

The name of Limerick has also been associated with the well known tobacco called Limerick Twist. This favourite article with smokers has had also to strive against foreign competition, and it has done so successfully. It is still a leading manufacture and is maintaining its well earned prestige. A large number of tanneries formerly existed in the city, but only two, those of Messrs E. O'Callaghan and Son, and Messrs W.J. O'Donnell are still holding their ground. The many breweries and distilleries of a hundred years ago are now represented by Mr Walker's distillery at Thomondgate.

The extensive army clothing establishment founded by Sir Peter Tait about twenty years ago has passed through strange vicissitudes. At the present time it is in full operation and gives employment to about one thousand hands.

A new industry has lately been established by the Condensed Milk Company of Ireland, which has already won its way into universal favour. Without doubt Limerick ought to be able to produce as fine condensed milk as any country in the world, lying as it does adjacent to an unrivalled pasture district, and it is gratifying to know that the Limerick Condensed Milk has already taken its place beside the best products of Switzerland. The firm has lately purchased the splendid premises at Lansdowne already referred to, where employment is given to four hundred hands and the milk of about ten thousand cows is utilized.

Several industries have however totally disappeared of recent years. The celebrated fishing hooks are no more to be met with, an inferior but cheaper article taking their place. Paper making has departed to other centres. Wood combing has followed its example. Limerick Gloves which were formerly sold enclosed in walnut shells are hardly even remembered. The Limerick Lace manufacture introduced by Mr Walker in 1829 had succeeded so wonderfully that no less than seventeen hundred persons were employed in 1841. Limerick Lace was famed throughout the world as one of the most beautiful articles of female adornment, receiving the approbation of royalty. Now, unhappily, the industry has greatly declined. It is still successfully cultivated by the Sisters of the Good Shepherd Convent, whose case at the last Art Exhibition in Limerick contained many beautiful specimens remarkable for their richness of design and carefulness of execution. Mrs R.V. O'Brien has recently taken this decaying industry in hand and has established a Lace Factory at Bank Place, the pupils of which have already produced some excellent specimens from designs by local artists, students of the School of Art.

The chief thoroughfare of Limerick is George Street, which, with the exception of Sackville Street, is the finest street in Ireland. The 'monster' Drapery establishments are at the northern extremity.

St. John's Cathedral.

These belong to Messrs. Cannock & Co., Messrs McBirney & Co., and the Limerick Warehouse Company. That of Messrs Todd & Co. is in William Street. In Patrick Street the Spirit establishments are examples of tasteful and costly architecture. Cruise's Hotel was well known in the early part of this century, being patronised by Daniel O'Connell, and it has ever since maintained its reputation.

Among modern edifices which ornament the city the first place must be assigned to St. John's Cathedral. Early in 1856 a meeting of the parishioners was held for the purpose of collecting funds to erect a new Cathedral to replace the old Chapel of St. John. Subscriptions poured in with such rapidity that the foundation stone was laid on the 1st of May that year. In a short space of time the building was open for worship, but the spire was not completed till 1883. The spire, which is 280 feet in height, was constructed from designs by Messrs M. and S. Hennessy, and is the most remarkable feature of the edifice. It is singularly graceful and light, and may be considered the loftiest and most beautiful in Ireland and as having but few rivals elsewhere. The internal length of the Cathedral is 168 feet, and the height to the apex of the roof eighty feet. The high altar, executed by a Belgian artist is the gift of Mrs. F. MacNamara, in memory of her husband. A beautiful statue of the Blessed Virgin in white marble, by Belzoni, was presented by Lord Emly.

St. John's Church is near the Cathedral, and was erected in 1843 on the site of the old Church, whose foundation dated probably from the 15th century. The Church contains many memorial windows erected to members of the Pery, Russell, Maunsell, and Corneille families. The wall surrounding the burial ground was built, as an inscription testifies, by the parishioners in 1693, during the mayoralty of John Foord, the promoter of the work. There are several very ancient tombs bearing curious sculptures. One near the entrance bears the device of a slipper, another the cock, thirty pieces of silver, etc.

At the southern end of the city and having the advantage of an elevated situation is the Redemptorist Church of St. Alphonsus. The foundation was laid in 1859, and the Church was dedicated in 1862. The style is early Gothic and the window over the entrance consists of five long lancets. The church is a little longer than St. John's Cathedral, being 173 feet in length and from the ridge of the roof to the floor the height is seventy-five feet. The late Mr John Quin was a munificent donor. The reredos and high altar, remarkably beautiful specimens of ecclesiastical art, are his gifts, and the lofty and massive tower with its peal of bells was erected at his expense. Mount Saint Vincent Convent and Orphanage are on the Military Road, presenting a large and handsome pile of buildings, ornamented with a small but remarkably beautiful spire.

It would exceed the limits within which we have confined ourselves to particularise the efforts made to enlarge and beautify the various churches of all denominations in Limerick. It must suffice to say that they are all worthy of the object for which they have been erected, and that no other city of the same size in the empire can exhibit so many beautiful and costly examples of the highest style of ecclesiastical architecture. The merchants of Limerick have not been found wanting in giving support to the various institutions in connection with the several churches to which they belong. Indeed they are deserving of every praise for the liberality with which they have supported every good and pious work.

The public monuments of Limerick commemorate many names of more than a local celebrity. The Park and Square were formed by subscription in memory of Mr Richard Russell, the ground being the gift of Lord Limerick. The Park has lately been enlarged and opened to the general public. It is tastefully planted and laid out and is a great boon to the neighbourhood. From the centre arises a tall column surmounted by a statue erected about the year 1830 to the Right Hon Thomas Spring Rice, first Lord Monteagle, who represented the city in Parliament from 1820 to 1833, and held the office of Chancellor of the Exchequer from 1835 to 1839.

Sir Peter Tait's energy and enterprise have been recognised by a public clock standing on a lofty pedestal of ornamented stonework, erected in 1867 in Baker Place, on the way to the Railway Station. The beautiful front of the Dominican Church is on one hand and on the other are the Havergal Memorial Hall and the Protestant Orphan Hall.

Statue of Daniel O'Connell in The Crescent.

In the centre of the Crescent stands a noble statue of O'Connell by Hogan, an eminent sculptor, which was inaugurated with appropriate ceremony in 1857, during the mayoralty of Dr Kane. A very fine portrait of the Liberator, by Haverty, hangs in the Council Chamber of the Town Hall, where may also be found a portrait of Mr William Fitzgerald, Mayor of Limerick in 1860, who died during his year of office.

In 1857 a monument was erected at the Wellesley Bridge 'to commemorate the bravery of Viscount Fitzgibbon, 8th Royal Irish Hussars, and of his gallant companions in arms, natives of the County and City of Limerick, who gloriously fell in the Crimean war'. The statue of Lord Fitzgibbon is life size and of bronze, and stands on a granite pedestal. On the front of the pedestal is a bass relief of the famous cavalry charge at Balaclava, in which Lord Fitzgibbon fell.

At the Clare end of Thomond Bridge is the Treaty Stone, on which it is popularly supposed the treaty of 1691 was signed in the presence of the English and Irish armies. The stone stands on a granite pedestal erected in 1865 by Mr. John Rickard Tinsley, Mayor, during that year. On the side of the pedestal are the city arms with the very appropriate motto, *urbs antiqua fuit studiisque asperrima belli*, words used by the Latin poet in reference to ancient Carthage, and which are exceedingly applicable to Limerick. The later history of our city shows that the omitted words *dives opum*, 'rich in resources', may also be added.

The last public monument erected in Limerick is the very fine statue of Patrick Sarsfield, the Irish Bayard, a chevalier *sans peur et sans reproche*. The project had been started as long ago as 1845, and a committee appointed. After considerable delay the statue was at last executed, and then a long controversy arose as to the site. The discussion was cut short by the statue being placed without any ceremony in its present position, where nobody sees it. A more prominent public situation would have been desirable and should have been obtained. The sculptor was Mr John Lawlor, of London, late of Dublin, who executed the group 'Engineering' on the Albert Memorial in Kensington Gardens. The founders were Young & Co., Pimlico, London. The bronze is of the best quality and it is considered the cheapest, as it is one of the best statues ever erected, the total cost being £1,077 1s 7d. On the front of the pedestal is the following inscription – 'To commemorate the indomitable energy and stainless honour of General Patrick Sarsfield, Earl of Lucan, the heroic defender of Limerick during the sieges of 1690 and 1691, who died from the effect of wounds received at the battle of Landen, 1693. This site was granted by the Most Reverend George Butler, Lord Bishop of Limerick, to the Trustees, Ambrose Hall, J.P., Robert V. O'Brien, William Spillane, J.P. Erected 1881.'

CHAPTER IX

The Neighbourhood of Limerick

IN THE NEIGHBOURHOOD OF LIMERICK are still to be found some very interesting ruins which have escaped complete destruction. Many others have been swept away, and in some cases only two or three large stones are left by chance to mark the spot where some ancient church or castle stood. Near the railway bridge on the road to Castlepark there was formerly a castle, which is marked on the ordnance maps, but it requires a close scrutiny now to detect any trace of its foundation. The old Castle of the Knights Templars, near Mungret, existed in fair preservation till about thirty years ago, but not a fragment of it can be pointed out at the present time. Nothing remains even to suggest an inquiry but the name of a residence close by called Temple Mungret. About a mile beyond Friarstown, on the road to Fedamore, a few large stones still held together by the tenacious mortar of olden times, tell of another stronghold which escaped the storms of war only to fall into the hands of a more ruthless destroyer.

Some few of these buildings were destroyed of set purpose, others have been allowed to crumble away, but more generally that decay has been accelerated by the owner or somebody else taking out the cut and squared limestone for the purpose of utilizing the material in the construction of a farm building or an outhouse. When this is done the rain and frost accomplish the rest.

Of those which have escaped total destruction the ruins of the once famous Abbey of Mungret attract particular attention. Situated within a short distance of the city they are easy of access and are well known. The most conspicuous building consists of three unequal portions communicating one with another by means of low square doorways. The east window is a long narrow lancet and the others are of the same character. A small tower with battlemented top rises above the walls, but the internal staircase has been destroyed. To the east of this,the principal structure at present, is a small chapel of earlier date. It is fourteen feet wide, but its length cannot be ascertained, as the wall of one of the gables is modern, and may not occupy the exact position of the original, which it replaces. The most ancient building of the three is the Monastic Church standing roofless by the roadside. According to O'Donovan it is built in the style of the 10th century, but other writers with more probability assign it to an earlier period. Like most of the ancient Irish churches it is a plain rectangle, without aisles or chancel. It measures forty-one feet in length by twenty-three in width, and the walls are fourteen high. In the east gable is a rude round-headed window, and there were two others. The door is placed in the west wall. It has a square top and is wider above than below. The huge lintel is split in the middle either from the weight of the gable above it, or the injury may have been caused by the action of fire during some of the conflagrations from which the Abbey suffered. At the lowest computation the building is a thousand years old and may be one or two centuries older, yet the stonework is so excellent that it looks as if it could stand for as long more. There were three other churches, but even their position cannot be pointed out, so completely have they been wrecked. In the adjacent fields may be observed straight mounds raised very slightly above the level of the sod, which look as if they marked the foundation of buildings, and suggest that the establishment was originally of considerable extent.

The Abbey of Mungret was founded in the 6th century by St. Nessan, whose death, according to the annals of the Four Masters, took place in 551. The Psalter of Cashel, which was compiled in the 9th century from more ancient records, states that it had within its walls six churches, and contained exclusive of scholars, fifteen hundred religious, of whom five hundred were learned preachers, five hundred psalmists, and five hundred employed in constant religious exercises. The story of the 'wise women of Mungret' cannot be omitted. The monks of Mungret were famed far and wide for their learning, so much so as to excite the curiosity of the professors of Lismore, or as others say, Cashel, who formed the design of coming and seeing for themselves if the reputation was well founded. The scholars of Mungret did not desire to risk their fame in a disputation which was not of their seeking but which they could not decline. They contrived a plan by which they escaped the inquisitive strangers and even still further enhanced their reputation. Some of the younger monks dressed themselves as washerwomen, and as the visitors approached, appeared vigorously washing clothes by the roadside. The Doctors inquired from them the way to the Abbey of Mungret, and to their astonishment were answered in various learned languages, spoken with perfect accuracy and precision. The strangers hesitated, and after a brief consultation came to the conclusion that if the very washerwomen of Mungret knew so much the monks and professors must know a vast deal more, and should they persist in their investigation, they themselves would only expose their own comparative ignorance in an intellectual encounter. So they returned home again and left the monks of Mungret alone.

The monastery suffered very much both from the Danes and the Irish. According to the annals of the Four Masters it was burned to the ground in 820, 834, and again in 840, by the Danes in their plundering excursions. The annals of Innisfallen record its destruction by Donald MacLaughlin and the men of Tyrconnell and Tyrone in 1088, and not long after it was plundered by Murtagh O'Brien in 1107. In 1194 King Donald O'Brien granted the lands of Mungret to the Bishop of Limerick, his successors, and the clergy of St. Mary's Cathedral, after which we meet with no further record of the Abbey.[1]

More ancient even than the oldest buildings of Mungret, one of the very first Christian churches ever erected in this country, is that of Donaghmore, which is situated within a few hundred yards of the Cork road, and about a mile and a half from the city. The edifice bears all the marks of a remote antiquity. The enclosed space is very small in extent and is simply rectangular. The door is in the west gable and as usual wider below than it is above, and the lintel is nearly seven feet long by three feet deep and two and a half thick. So far it very much resembles the church at Mungret. Further evidence of its antiquity is however forthcoming and refers it back to times which witnessed the early dawn of Christianity, and connect it with the Apostle of Ireland. There are reasons for referring its foundation to the time of St. Patrick's visit to Singland, and perhaps the Saint's own hand traced its simple lines. 'According to the Tripartite life, Jocelin Ussher, &c., all the Churches that bear the name of *Domhnach*, or in the anglicised form, Donagh, were originally founded by St. Patrick; and they were so called because he marked out their foundations on Sunday'.[2] The Irish word *Domhnach*, pronounced Downagh, signifies both a church and Sunday. The evidence then seems conclusive which ascribes its foundation to St. Patrick. The time that this little building, measuring externally forty feet by twenty-six, could have received the name of Donaghmore, the Great Church, must have been remote indeed. Almost the whole of the east wall is modern. There are only two windows at present existing. That in the east gable is a narrow slit, not in the middle of the wall, but situated a little to the right. The second window was in the south wall near the west end, but the interior of it is very much injured and looks more like a hole than a window. The adjacent burial ground was the place of sepulture of many distinguished Irish families, and particularly of the Clan Ua Conail, whose name is still preserved in the designation of the two Baronies of Upper and Lower Connello. In 1853 John George O'Connell was buried here at midnight and by torchlight, according to the custom of his family, and an inscription on his tomb speaks of him as being 'the last of his race'.

The historical references to Donaghmore are very few. The name occurs in the list of dignities established by Bishop Donat in connection with St. Mary's Cathedral, and again in a taxation of the see and of the chapter, made in 1291, by authority of Pope Innocent IV. At what time the church ceased to be used for divine service we have not been able to discover.

Half a mile from Donaghmore is the small square tower of Rathurd, built on or near the site of the ancient fort of Rath-arda-Suird. This

114

Newgate Brewery, established in 1831, and once one of the largest in Ireland.

rath, according to the annals of the Four Masters, was erected in the year of the world 3501 by Suird, one of the early Milesian invaders.

The old fortified residence known as Newcastle is said with little probability, to have been occupied by King William during the seige of 1690. It was not the habit of that general to place an impassable morass between himself and his army. Nothing is known of the erection of Newcastle, it was probably one of the many edifices of the kind which sprang up in the latter part of the 15th century.[4]

A similar oblivion rests upon the name of the builder of Castle Troy, so picturesquely situated by the banks of the Shannon, and commanding what in dry seasons was a ford of that river. In Lewis's *Topographical Dictionary* its erection is attributed to Dermot O'Brien in the reign of Henry III, but no authority is given for the statement. In the reign of Charles II Castle Troy was granted amongst other places to James, Duke of York. Before that time it was the property of Baron Bourke, of Brittas, and was rented to a Mackeogh, of Clonkeen.[5]

To the south and south east of the city may be noticed Tuoreen Castle, near the banks of the Groody, Drombanny Castle, a tall square tower, and Lickadoon Castle, once the seat of the O'Hurleys, now little more than a shapeless heap of stones. Lickadoon Castle is mentioned in *Pacata Hibernia* as one of the fortified stations in which a strong detachment was placed on the subjugation of the eastern part of the county in 1600. The hill of Friarstown hard by contains no less than five large earthen forts in good preservation. There are also the remains, still in a fair state of preservation, of the monastic establishment founded by the Clangibbon family, which gave its name to the place. A castle and church stood on the eastern side of the hill, but nothing is known regarding them. A third castle, Fanningstown, founded by the Fitzgeralds, on the way towards Fedamore has disappeared all but a few stones.

In the low lying boggy ground west of Friarstown, and midway between it and the large earthen moat on Green Hills, may be observed a fort whose shape is not circular but rectangular, or rather pentagonal, as one side is bent so as to form two. The fort is eighty paces long by forty-five wide. It is surrounded by a double rampart and seems to have been connected with other structures in the neighbourhood, which cannot now be distinctly traced. The very unusual shape however is the chief characteristic which deserves mention. All the neighbourhood contains numerous chains of forts, and evidently this was the usual route from Limerick to the western parts of the county. Fitzgerald relates that in a place called the Camp Field, a peasant, whilst digging in the Summer of 1821, found what he calls a 'gold crown' in the form of a large oystershell, weighing 5½ ounces. The crown was unfortunately sold to a Dublin goldsmith for sixteen pounds and probably melted.

The most striking and picturesque ruin is that of Carrig-o-Gunnell, situated five miles to the west of the city. A short ridge of dolomite rock breaks through the surrounding limestone and varies the undulating surface. The northern extremity of the ridge ends in a steep broken crag, picturesque in its ruggedness, and is surmounted by the remains of a fine old castle. Seen from the city it stands 'bosomed high in tufted trees', whilst from other directions the walls can hardly be distinguished from the rock upon which they are erected. Viewed from such a distance that the eye can take in castle and rock and river, one is forcibly reminded of that 'castled crag' which 'frowns o'er the wide and winding Rhine'. Nor is the resemblance between the two in appearance only. Like the Drachenfels Carrig has its legend, not exactly of a dragon dwelling in an enchanted cave, but of a bull breathing forth sulphurous flames, who long ago fixed his dwelling on the rock, where he issued forth at frequent intervals to ravage the surrounding country. The scourge was intolerable but at last a deliverer appeared in the person of St. Patrick. The Saint sought him in his hiding place, whence he fled as far as Adare, followed by St. Patrick in close pursuit, and was there drowned in an unsuccessful attempt to reach the other side of the Maigue, no evil thing having the power to cross running water.

Another legend tells of a witch who, night after night raised her magic candle upon the summit of the crag, and such was the nature of its beams that whosoever saw a glimmer of her enchanted light was sure to die within the next twelve months.

117

Hence it was said the rock was called 'The Rock of the Candle'.

A more correct knowledge of the original spelling of the name does away however with all attempts to connect the rock with any magic light, whether of the witch or the fire-breathing bull. The correct title is not Carraig-an-Coinneal, which would indeed mean the Rock of the Candle, but Carraig-O-gCoinneal, which signifies nothing more or less than the Rock of the O'Connells, to whom the adjacent territories once belonged. The O'Connells were dispossessed at an early date, but the connection of this family with the County Limerick is still preserved in the names of the two Baronies of Upper and Lower Connello. Donogh O'Brien obtained the Lordship of Carrig-o-Gunnell from King John, in 1210, and was the first of his family who used the name O'Brien in preference to the royal title of King of Thomond. It is thought that from him the adjacent territory got its baronial title of Pubble Brien, or O'Brien's People.

When or by whom the present structure was erected we have not been able to discover. Doubtless from the earliest times a stronghold of some kind or another must have existed on this important and commanding site. The Irish Dun or Cashel after the Norman invasion, was replaced by a strong fortress more in keeping with the warlike necessities of the times. The fortress whose ruins now crown the rock has been ascribed to the great order of Military Monks, the Knights Templars, who acquired such renown in the 13th century. If the statement be correct, and there is no reason for doubting its accuracy, the black and white flag of the Templars seldom floated above the turrets of a more stately structure.

On the suppression of the order in 1312 the building appears to have been acquired by the O'Briens, who, whilst the Normans were gradually ousting the ancient families out of their possessions, seem to have been quite secure within the walls of Carrig. It is not till the reign of Henry VIII that we read of any successful attempt to expel them and secure the castle for the English King.

At this period Conor O'Brien held the Principality of Thomond. The next heir should have been his son, Donogh, who had allied himself by marriage with the house of Ormond, a family which warmly supported the English interest. Dissensions having arisen in the household of Conor O'Brien, the young prince endeavoured to push his own interests by means of the powerful nobles with whom he was allied. Donogh accordingly went to meet his brother-in-law, Lord James Butler, then at Adare, and made a remarkable speech which we find recorded in a letter from Lord James to Thomas Cromwell.

The Irish prince is reported to have said – 'I have married your sister, and because I have married your sister I have forsaken my father, my uncle, and all my friends and my country to come to you to help to do the King's service. I have been sore wounded and I have no reward nor anything to live upon. What would you have me to do? If it would please the King's grace to take me into his service, and that you will come into the country and bring with you a piece of ordnance to win a castle called Carrig-o-Gunnell, and his grace to give me that which was never in English possession for two hundred years, and I will desire the King no help nor aid of any man but this English Captain with his hundred and odd Englishmen to go with me upon my father and my uncle, the which are the King's enemies, and upon the Irish who were never among Englishmen, and if I do hurt or harm, or if there be any mistrust, I will put in pledge as good as ye require, that I will hurt no Englishman, but upon the wild Irishmen that are the King's enemies. And for all such land as I shall conquer it shall be at the King's pleasure to set Englishmen in it, to be held at the King's pleasure. And I too shall refuse all such Irish fashions, and to order myself after the English laws and all that I can make or conquer.'

This very peculiar but perhaps at the time not unusual proposal exactly suited the views of the English leaders, who on the cessation of the wars of the Roses had turned their attention towards the more complete subjugation of the South of Ireland. On the very next day after the above speech was made by Donogh the English forces marched from Adare under the command of Lord Grey, the Deputy of Ireland. The Deputy in a despatch to Thomas Cromwell states that on his appearance before the castle he 'fell a parleying with the

Constable thereof, which I found very strait and hard, with many high words unto me, and in no wise would hear it until I had laid my artillery and men around it, and then came to an appointment with me to let me have it, so that I would let him and his depart with bag and baggage'. The terms were agreed to by the council, especially as the arrangement would 'spare powder and shot and other divers things which we should have lacked at other several times when we should have done other great affairs'. On the evacuation of the fortress, Lord Grey, The Earl of Ossory, The Lord Chancellor, and others, entered and viewed their new acquisition. The royal standard was borne by Lord Dudley and the Mayor of Limerick. On the departure of those noblemen for Limerick a garrison was left in charge.

Whilst the Deputy and Lord James were planning how they could contrive to keep their pledge to Donogh and at the same time secure Carrig to the King, news reached them that the castle fell again into the hands of the rightful owner 'by tradiment,' and was now manned by gunners and soldiers of the Earl of Desmond and O'Brien.

Grey marched at once to recover the castle, before which he appeared on the 15th August, 1536. A summons to unconditional surrender being rejected, 'the ordnance was bent upon one of the gates of the base court, whereat such a battery was made, as after by strength of men, the King's Deputy won the base court, in achieving which certain of his retinue of Englishmen were slain and others sore hurted. That done the ordnance was bent upon the donjon of the great castle, and after a convenient battery made, divers assaults were bravely given by the Englishmen, wherein they were resisted and divers of them slain, and others sore hurted. Nevertheless the next night following a company of the Lord Deputy's retinue entered in the night into a tower in the castle, keeping the same until it was daylight, at which time others of the army entered likewise, and so finally won the whole garrison with all the persons that were therein to the number of forty-six, besides thirteen which were slain with our ordnance and four with our arrows at the said assaults made, whom before the entry of the castle the others had burnt. And because the

Lord Deputy before any siege laid to the said castle, did give summons to him to surrender to him the house, or else in case they should hold the same and kill any of the army, if he did afterwards win it, all that were therein should die; which so had, all the said persons were put to death accordingly, except a certain of the chief of them, being gentlemen of the O'Briens (for the redemption of whose life both great intercession was made, and good sums of money offered,) which being conveyed by us to the city of Limerick the Lord Deputy caused to be arraigned according to the King's laws and after to be executed as traitors attainted of high treason. The dread and example of which we trust shall be a means that few garrisons in Munster shall be kept against the King's Deputy, especially if they perceive that he have great ordnance with him.'

The gunners are said to have done their part 'wondrously well', and the commander 'both about the order of the ordnance and the putting forward and animating of the soldiers, showed himself to be an active and bold gentleman'. In this enterprise of the English there were 'killed, sore hurt and wounded', about thirty men, which shows that the garrison must have been greatly outnumbered by the besiegers and that the resistance was very determined.

Conor O'Brien died in 1539 and was succeeded by Morrogh, the Tanist, who according to the usages of tanistry, was installed King of Thomond. Morrogh joined a league of the Irish Chiefs against Henry VIII but the confederacy could effect nothing of importance and very soon dissolved. The King of Thomond abandoned further resistance to Henry, whom he now acknowledged as his Sovereign. He resigned his royal claims and in their stead accepted the title of Earl of Thomond for life, with remainder to his nephew, Donogh, but superadded to the limited dignity was the Barony of Inchiquin in tail. Murrogh and his nephew were invested with the insignia of their rank at Greenwich on 1st July, 1543.[6]

Thus passed away the kingly title founded by Brian Boru. It was not till 1551 that Donogh succeeded to his uncle's titles and possessions, amongst the latter being Carrig-o-Gunnell, for which he had schemed so long and so unsuccessfully. This district remained in the hands of the O'Briens till 1641, when it was forfeited to the Crown, and at the Restoration was granted to Michael Boyle, Archbishop of Dublin.[7]

Conor O'Brien, who died in 1539, was ancestor of the Earls of Thomond and Viscounts Clare. The eighth and last Earl of Thomond died in 1741. Daniel was created Viscount Clare in 1662. The third Viscount fought at the Boyne for James II and was outlawed. His famous regiment, Clare's Dragoons, was one of the most distinguished of the Irish Brigades. The title became extinct in 1774. The Marquisate of Thomond created in 1808 expired in 1855, on which occasion the Barony of Inchiquin, conferred on Murrogh three hundred and thirteen years before, passed from the descendants of his eldest son, Dermot, to Sir Lucius O'Brien, the representative of his third son, Donogh of Lemenagh. The present Lord Inchiquin is therefore the representative of Brian Boru and of Olioll Ollum, who reigned over Munster in the 2nd century of our era.

Carrig-o-Gunnell is not mentioned during the exciting times of 1641-1651, though its neighbour, Bunratty, on the opposite shore, attracted considerable attention and was twice besieged.

In 1691, previous to the last siege of Limerick, it was held by a small party of Irish soldiers, who surrendered to General Sgavenmore, and their place was supplied by an English garrison. Shortly afterwards both it and Castle-Connell were blown up with gunpowder by order of Ginkle, under the supervision of Story, Dean of Limerick. The present condition of the building shows how completely the work of destruction was carried out.

The ruins of Carrig-o-Gunnell occupy a considerable extent of ground and there are also traces of outworks at some distance from the walls. Entrance to the enclosure may be obtained at several places, but the easiest mode of access is through a small gate at the south east angle. This was evidently the chief entrance to the courtyard, and the stone bench for the accommodation of the guard is still in good preservation. Just outside the gate on the right hand side, about seven feet from the ground, may be observed a stone which had been struck and splintered by a cannon shot. From a spot in the centre a star-like

122

Opening of the floating docks in Limerick by the Lord-Lieutenant.

series of cracks spreads in all directions. It is very likely this shot was fired at the siege of 1536, when 'the ordnance was bent upon one of the gates of the base court'.

To the left of the entrance is a huge breach, but the intervening wall has not suffered, and is of considerable height. Near the base it is pierced by a single and again by a double porthole. The aperture at the acute angle very like a door was originally much smaller and served as a look-out. To the right of the entrance the wall has suffered very severely. In the far corner may be observed the remains of the great hall, twenty-seven paces in length by seven in width. The eastern end is not exactly square. Indeed the outer wall is of no regular shape and was evidently constructed so as to take advantage of the conformation of the rock. The surface of the courtyard is very uneven and rugged, and the Templars must have been excellent horsemen to be able to guide their fiery chargers over its slippery rocks. From the entrance to the main buildings there is a path leading up the slight ascent. At present the track lies between huge masses of masonry, the broken and shattered fragments of the original entrance to the inner court of the castle. To judge from the indications that can now be discovered this must have been an exceedingly strong position, absolutely impregnable before the days of gunpowder and perhaps for long after. A lofty round tower containing a spiral stone staircase surmounted the works at this point, though its exact position cannot be defined. It is very probable that it stood over the entrance, for it does not fit in with any of the buildings the foundation of which can be traced. A considerable fragment of the tower, eight feet in length, may be observed close at hand, with the staircase still intact, but turned upside down. The explosion which demolished the defence at this point rent the tower asunder, flung this piece aloft unbroken, and turning over in mid air the fragment fell where it is today, the masonry still solid as a rock and like the well known broken tower of Heidelberg Castle, uninjured by its aerial somersault. Another very large breach has been made in the walls and buildings of the inner court, and the ground is strewn with the wreck of what appears to have been the domestic apartments. The castle proper or 'donjon' as it was called on page 120, is still in very good preservation, and the staircase leading to the top is almost perfect. One of the chief dwelling houses stood adjacent to it, but nothing now remains except a gable containing windows and fireplaces, by which a fair idea of what it once was can easily be obtained. This dwelling was connected with the keep by a doorway in the under storey, but the regular entrance was on the second floor. Exterior to the main building may be observed the foundation of a round tower, and judging from the indications on the adjacent walls, it was so constructed that those in the round tower could at will cut off communication with the keep.

The view from the summit of the castle is very extensive, embracing the greater part of the County Limerick, with portions of Clare and Tipperary. Far to the west may be observed the estuary of the Fergus, diminished by perspective to a silver thread and above it the hills extending inland from Kilrush and terminating with the broad flat summit of Mount Callan, their highest point. On the opposite shore are 'Bunratty's royal walls', founded by de Clare in 1272. The castle is now a police barrack. On the Clare hills are the dark woods of Cratloe, the remnants of the ancient oak forests, whose timbers constructed the ships which destroyed the Spanish Armada. In Summer time the white tents of the encampment on Woodcock hill stand out clear against the heathery background. The course of the Shannon can be traced up to the towers and spires of Limerick, conspicuous amongst which are the dark massive turrets of St. Mary's Cathedral, the tall slender shaft of St. John's Cathedral and the more bulky spire of the Redemptorist Church. The rounded dome of Keeper Hill rises two thousand three hundred feet above the plain, and continuing the line of the Slieve Phelim mountains the observer comes to the Galtee range, whose highest point is over three thousand feet in height. Across the south of the panorama stretch the Ballyhoura mountains, whose eastern summit, Seefin, preserves the name of the celebrated hero, Finn, the son of Cumhal. Then the eye glances to the conical summit of Knockfierna and the view is bounded on the west by the range which extends from the borders of Cork to Knockpatrick, overlooking the Shannon. On the summit of a slight depression, clearly visible against the sky-line, may be remarked the low frowning mass which is all that remains of the famous stronghold of Shanid, whose name supplied the battle cry of the Desmonds. The course of the 'winding Maigue' justifies the epithet applied to it. Lord Limerick's beautiful modern mansion is conspicuous on a hill to the west, whilst Elm Park, the seat of Lord Clarina, and Tervoe, that of Lord Emly, may both be observed in their well-wooded demesnes.

Carrig is a famous holiday resort of the citizens of Limerick. It is within a convenient distance of the city and is easy of access. The ruins which crown the rock never lose their charm, whilst the view, either from the breaches in the walls, or better still that from the top of the tower, is a panorama of unrivalled beauty, with its magnificent distances. As the citizen gazes from the summit of the old fortress upon the gray old city by the Shannon shore perhaps his interest may not be lessened nor his pleasure diminished by possessing even a slight knowledge of the events connected with Limerick and its Sieges.

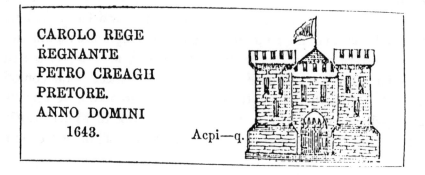

CAROLO REGE
REGNANTE
PETRO CREAGH
PRETORE.
ANNO DOMINI
1643.

Acpi—q.

APPENDIX

A. King's Castle. B. Cathedral. C. The Watch-House on yᵉ Bridge. D. Thomond Bridge. E. Shannon River.

Limerick City Militia

The following sketch appeared in the *Limerick Chronicle* of 13th May, 1882, at the time the name of the Regiment was changed to that of the 'Fourth Brigade, South Irish Division Royal Artillery':

The Limerick City Regiment of Militia was raised early in 1793 as an infantry regiment. John Prendergast Smyth, M.P., (afterwards Viscount Gort) then commander of the 'Limerick Independents', was appointed by the Lord Lieutenant, Colonel of the newly-raised body. In the month of May following the Field Officers were settled as follows:

Colonel – John Prendergast Smyth, M.P., First Viscount Gort.
Lieutenant-Colonel – Hon. E.H. Pery, First Earl of Limerick.
Major – Charles Vereker, M.P., Second Viscount Gort.

On the 7th of June the regiment was first called up. The establishment in 1794 was as follows:

1 Lieutenant-Colonel	1 Quarter-Master
1 Major	1 Surgeon
4 Captains	1 Adjutant
1 Captain-Lieutenant	1 Chaplain
6 Lieutenants	1 Sergeant-Major
5 Ensigns	1 Drum-Major

17 Sergeants, 18 Corporals, 13 Drummers, 255 Privates.

The Commissions of the following officers are all dated May, 1793:-

Captain – George Gough (afterwards Major and Lieutenant-Colonel).
Captain-Lieutenant – Samuel Tomkins (afterwards Major).
Adjutant – Henry Horsfall.

Lieutenant – John Waller (afterwards Adjutant).

Ensigns – Hugh Gough (afterwards First Viscount Gough and Field Marshal);

David Nash (afterwards Captain); Exham Moroney (afterwards Lieutenant); John Vereker.

In 1794, the following gentlemen received commissions as Ensigns: – John Friend, John Waller, William Marley, Richard Cripps, and William Bouchier.

The first route we find to have been from Limerick to Parsonstown shortly after they were enrolled. In that terrible year, 1798, the regiment was variously stationed in the province of Ulster, and was constantly employed in quelling disturbances there. We find one engagement with the insurgents mentioned. On the 6th of June, Lieutenant-Colonel Gough was ordered to march at eleven o'clock that night with a hundred men of the Limerick City Militia and sixty Cavalry to attack a rebel camp situated within six miles of Edenderry. He and his forces arrived at their destination at five o'clock next morning. The enemy, to the number of three hundred men, were strongly posted behind a quickset hedge, and their rere was protected by a bog, one of the detached parts of the Bog of Allen. The cavalry were ordered round by the right so as to get between them and the bog, and thus cut off their retreat. The cavalry, owing to the nature of the ground, were unable to execute this movement in time. Meanwhile the infantry with difficulty were making their way round the other flank. They had to climb ditches strongly barricaded with stakes interwoven with white thorn. Nevertheless they succeeded, and the rebels after firing a volley retreated to the bog hotly pursued. Gough finding they would not stand halted his men and poured a volley, which only had the effect of quickening their flight. They were pursued for five miles, and at length saved themselves from further pursuit by disappearing in the impassable morasses of the great Bog of Allen. It is satisfactory to know that not only was the attack of the Limerick men conducted with judgement and spirit but also not a single man received the slightest hurt.

On the landing of the French under General Humbert at Killala Bay, the regiment, under the command of Colonel Vereker, was ordered to Sligo. They had reached Carrick-on-Shannon when the disastrous defeat at Castlebar on the 27th of August occurred. Had the Limerick men been there the 'Castlebar Races' might have been run on a different course and by other riders. They marched on to Sligo, a large and important town, and reached it just in time. The French, elated by their victory, turned northwards from

Castlebar with the intention of taking Sligo, passing into Ulster, there to join a new force of invaders whose landing in some of the innumerable inlets of the County Donegal was daily expected. Humbert reached Colloony, a village seven English miles from Sligo, and Vereker and his men were ordered to evacuate the town and leave the inhabitants to the tender mercies of the French and the rebels.

Two rivers – the Owen More and the Owen Beg – join their streams a little distance from Coloony and at the village itself flow into the Arrow coming from the lake of the same name. These united rivers, over a rocky bed, plunge headlong over ledges and form numerous rapids. Its course northward is swift and short till at Ballisodare, after leaping the picturesque falls of that name, it empties itself into the deep inlet of Ballisodare Bay. A long range of hills extends from Lough Gill westward, almost at right angles to the course of the river, and reach to within a short distance of the river. These hills were well wooded then, as they are still, and in one spot reach an elevation of over nine hundred feet. The road from Colloony to Sligo passes by the side of the river for about a mile and a half. At Carrick-na-Gatt it turns round the extremity of the above-mentioned ridge. The remainder of the way to Sligo is over an open level country, and the distance is about five English miles.

When Colonel Vereker was ordered to evacuate Sligo and retire, he demanded before he did so to give Humbert battle. He skilfully chose his ground. He saw that at Carrick-na-Gatt he could dispose of his men so as to make as much of his little force as possible, and at the same time conceal the smallness of their number. Captain Vincent and a hundred men were sent as an advanced guard. He himself moved on with twenty dragoons, thirty yeomen cavalry, thirty yeomen infantry, twenty Essex Fencibles, two hundred and fifty Limerick City Militia, and two guns. The enemy numbered nine hundred French troops, two hundred and fifty of the Longford and Kerry Militia, who joined the invaders, a large body of rebels – by some authorities said to number three thousand – and nine pieces of cannon. Colonel Vereker took up his position at Carrick-na-Gatt. His left was protected by the river, his right rested on the hill. His guns were placed on the high road. The advanced guard, under Captain Vincent, was received by the enemy with a sharp fire, and Captain Waller and the Limerick Light Company were ordered to advance and support them. Major Ormsby and one company occupied a post on the hill at the left to support that flank. The battle began at half-past two in the afternoon and continued till after four. Major Ormsby's division on the hill supported the brunt of the attack. At last, when the ammunition was almost gone, overpowered by numbers, they had to give way.

The enemy rushed round in the rere, and Colonel Vereker, almost surrounded, had at length to draw off his men, leaving behind his two cannon, the artillery horses being so badly wounded that they were unable to bring them off. He was however able to carry off his ammunition waggon and harness. He crossed the river in good order, and returning to Sligo withdrew to Ballyshannon. The French retired eastward, along the southern base of the hills above mentioned, relinquishing their cannon on the way. This gallant action saved Sligo, and turned the French from Ulster. Humbert surrendered to Lord Cornwallis shortly after, and all danger from that quarter was at an end. Colonel Vereker reported his casualties at seven killed and twenty-two wounded. The French lost twenty-eight killed and about fifty wounded.

Ensign Rumley was killed in the engagement and Captain Cripps was severely wounded, shot through the neck and jaws. The three field officers were slightly wounded.

Nothing could exceed the enthusiasm with which all regarded this spirited action, and the gallant conduct of the little band and their leader. The thanks of the Irish Parliament, in most complimentary terms, were voted to Colonel Vereker and the Limerick heroes. Nor did George III omit to notice their deserts. He conferred on Colonel Vereker the privilege of bearing supporters and other honourable augmentations to his arms usually borne only by peers.

General Humbert is reported to have said when giving up his sword to Lord Cornwallis, 'I met many generals in Ireland, but the only soldier amongst them was Colonel Vereker.' The troops were received on their return home with the greatest enthusiasm. The Corporation marked their opinion by the following resolutions, dated 8th October, 1798:

Resolved – 'That the steady loyalty and gallant conduct of our fellow-citizens of the Limerick City Regiment of Militia, who on the 5th September last, under the command of Colonel Vereker, so intrepidly engaged and successfully opposed the progress of the whole French and rebel army at Colloony, merits our sincerest thanks and warmest applause, a conduct which has not only covered them as a regiment with eternal honours, but has also cast an additional lustre on this their native city, already so distinguished for its loyalty and zeal for our happy Constitution.'

Resolved – 'That the sum of fifty guineas be paid by our chamberlain towards raising a fund to purchase a suitable piece of Plate for the Officers' Mess, and proper Medals for such of the Non-commissioned Officers and

Privates of the regiment as were engaged in the action of that day.'

On the 5th of December following the Corporation also ordered the purchase of a sword of honour, to be presented to the colonel of the regiment by the mayor, and caused his description of the battle to be inserted on the minutes.

In 1801 the regiment was augmented to 460 men.

In August of the same year the regiment offered to extend its services to any part of the United Kingdom.

In May, 1802, after the delusive peace of Amiens the regiment was disembodied, but next year it again assembled, and in the month of October was inspected by Brigadier General Affleck, who reported very favourably of the Corps. During the Peninsular war we find the regiment quartered in various parts of Ireland. In 1804 the regiment was stationed at Ballinrobe, in July, 1805, at Boyle, and in the next month the headquarters were at Enniskillen. In January, 1806, the regiment was still further augmented by a hundred men. In the beginning of 1807 the headquarters were at Ballyshannon, in the following year at Cavan, thence they removed in June, 1809, to Naas, where they continued till the Spring of 1811, when they were in Dublin. In July, 1811, the regiment was thanked by H.R.H. the Duke of York for 'the zealous offer of their extended services', made by all the officers and nearly four hundred men. The regiment marched to Cavan, in June, 1812, when the following was the roll of officers:

Colonel – Charles Vereker.
Lieut.-Colonel – George Gough.
Majors – Samuel Tomkins and
John Prendergast Vereker.
Captains – John B. Westropp, John Vereker, Exham Moroney, David Nash, Eyre Powell, and Francis Butler.
Lieutenants – Thos. Ormsby, Norman Tomkins, Charles Maunsell, John Standish, William O'Dell, John Piercy, John F. Sargent, John Fitzgibbon, Daniel Smyth, Wm. Smithwick, Robert McCraith, Godfrey Massy, Henry D'Esterre.
Ensigns – Thomas Powell, Wm. Lloyd, Christopher Hemsworth, John Smith and John Westropp.
Paymaster – John Wallace.
Adjutant – John Waller.
Surgeon – William Gibson.
Assistant-Surgeon – Richard Burgess.

Quarter-Master – James de B. Morris.

In May, 1813, the regiment proceeded to Cork, and remained there till the disembodiment of the Irish Militia, consequent upon the peace of Fontainbleau and the abdication of Napoleon. The regiment marched to Limerick, and dispersed in July, 1814. A mutiny very nearly resulted in consequence of a penurious Government not allowing the men to take their great coats with them, the coats being required by the Government to clothe the ragged heroes coming home from the Peninsula.

On 18th July, 1815, the regiment was again embodied. Only one major was, however, allowed on the permanent staff, and Major Tomkins was elected to serve. The headquarters proceeded to Kinsale and Charlesfort in the months of August and September, and remained there until again disembodied on the 22nd March, 1816, in Limerick. The privates then numbered 493. On the decease of Lieutenant-Colonel Gough in 1837, the Hon Charles Smyth Vereker succeeded him as Lieutenant-Colonel, and the Hon Standish Prendergast Vereker succeeded Major Tomkins in the Majority in 1842. On the 7th December of the latter year John Prendergast, third Viscount Gort, who had served in the regiment as major during its second embodiment, succeeded his father as colonel.

In the year 1854, in consequence of war breaking out with Russia, and in compliance with the provisions of the new Militia Act, the City of Limerick Regiment was changed from being an infantry into being an artillery corps. It was to consist of three companies of 234 rank and file, and recruiting began on 10th November of that year. The regiment had its full quota of men, and was again embodied on 3rd February, 1855. The following officers then held commissions:

Colonel – Viscount Gort.
Major and Commandant – Hon Standish P. Vereker.
Captains – Ralph Westropp and Thomas Royce.
Lieutenant —Charles Smyth.
Adjutant—William Phillips.
Surgeon – William D. Murphy.
First Lieutenants – John Fitzgibbon and Walker Mahony.
Second Lieutenants – George D. Furlong and Francis Morony.
Quarter-Master – Christopher Neary.

The regiment marched from Limerick to Kinsale (where it had been stationed forty years before) on the 28th September, 1855, and from Kinsale to Youghal on the 6th of December following, furnishing a detachment to garrison Carlisle Fort, which commands the entrance to Cork harbour. Whilst stationed in Youghal during the month of May a disastrous fire broke out in the main street, and at one time seriously threatened the existence of the whole town. By the tremendous efforts of the Limerick Militia its ravages were arrested and the fire subdued. The Youghal Town Council passed a hearty vote of thanks to the regiment for their conduct on that occasion, mentioning that the greater portion of the town would have been consumed but for their exertions.

Again, whilst the regiment was assembled for training, in May, 1860, a most extensive fire occurred at the business premises of J. & G. Boyd, William Street, and again the artillery coped successfully with its ravages. At a meeting of the Town Council on the 7th of May, Wm. Fitzgerald, Mayor, in the chair, the following resolution was proposed by T.C. Carte, and seconded unanimously.

Resolved – 'That the thanks of the Corporation are due and hereby given to the Honourable Col. Vereker, City Artillery, and officers and men of the same corps, for the active and energetic exertions on the occasion of the recent great fire in the city, at the concerns of J. & G. Boyd, William Street, and through whose zealous co-operation with the magistrates and citizens the spread of the destructive element was prevented, and the property adjoining of the several citizens saved.

(Signed) W. Fitzgerald, Mayor.'

In accordance with a circular dated Dublin Castle, 14th of August, 1860, the officers were permitted to wear the badge as worn by the Royal Artillery, but without the motto *Ubique.*

The regiment, owing to the state of the country, was not trained during the five years from 1866-1870 inclusive.

In 1872 orders were issued to increase the regiment by a hundred rank and file, twenty-two of whom were enrolled during the training.

A very pleasing incident occurred in 1873. The officers of the regiment during the training of 1872 and 1873 having availed themselves of the mess, kindly placed at their disposal by the officers of the 64th Regiment, subscribed and presented that regiment with a handsome clock bearing a suitable inscription. The officers of the 64th Regiment, in reply, said they would always preserve it as a friendly souvenir of the days spent together by the two regiments in the City of Limerick.

In 1874 the regiment was further increased by one battery, the number being 450 gunners, five trumpeters, twenty corporals, ten sergeants, ten sergeants permanent staff, and the usual complement of officers.

When the Reserve were mobilized in 1878, 156 men of this regiment served with the regular army, and were dismissed to their homes on 31st of July.

For a portion of this account, referring chiefly to the engagements of Edenderry and Colloony, we are indebted to the storehouse of information, Mr Lenihan's excellent history of Limerick. The lists of officers and other details have been obtained from the regimental records.

The present Officers (March, 1890) of the Limerick City Artillery are:

Colonel – Viscount Gort.
Lieutenant-Colonel – G.C. Spaight.
Instructor of Artillery – W.A. Bentley.
Adjutant – Captain Dallas.
Quarter-Master – J. Edwards.
Major – W.D. Maunsell.
Captains – W.A. Bentley, S.C.P. Vansittart, M. Westropp, J. Massy Westropp, A. Kershaw.
Lieutenants – W. De la F. Wright, H.E. Ayres, C. Lefroy, C. St. L. G. Hawkes, H.J. Hillyard, W.J. Ottley.
2nd Lieutenants – G.D. Wheeler, A.P. Berthon, J.J. Nicholson.

NOTES

CHAPTER I

1 From annals 4 M., 661.
   The Luimneach did not bear on its bosom of the race of Munster into Leath Chuinn.
   A corpse in a boat so precious as he, as Cummin, the son of Fiachna.
   In the *Book of Leinster* quoted by O'Donovan, Cuchullin is represented as standing on the top of Knockainey and pointing out the features of the country to his tutor. He says – The river Luimneach is that bright river that thou seest.
2 Mr James Frost informs me that until quite recently a large mound of stones existed upon the side of Glenagross mountain, and was called Leacht an Righ, the Tomb of the King.
3 St. Manchin was Abbot of the Church of Ennistymon, where he is still venerated as patron saint of the parish of Kilmanaheen (Cill Mainchinne). All that is known about St. Manchin will be found in Archdall's *Monasticon Hibernicum*, edited by Right Rev Dr Moran, Bishop of Ossory, in a very copious note on pp 82-85.

CHAPTER II

1 Besieged.—Ed

CHAPTER V

1 A temporary earthwork built inside a permanent fort as a last defensive position.—Ed
2 An Irish irregular soldier of the late 17th century.—Ed
3 The outer side of the ditch of a fort.—Ed

CHAPTER VI

1 A bundle of long sticks used in the construction of fortifications, embankments, etc.—Ed

CHAPTER VII

1 The author is describing Limerick as it was at the time of his writing (1890).—Ed
2 For a more detailed account the reader is referred to a handbook by the Rev F. Meredyth, Precentor, entitled *A Historic and Descriptive Sketch of St. Mary's Cathedral*. The present Dean, the Very Rev T. Bunbury, has done more to improve the Cathedral and its surroundings than has been accomplished by all other dignitaries in recent times.
3 Lenihan's *History of Limerick*, page 127.
4 Ibid, p. 289.
5 Annals of Innisfallen.

CHAPTER VIII

1 The author refers to Limerick in 1890.—Ed
    Whilst going through the press we learn that Dr. Courtenay has been appointed Inspector of
    Lunatic Asylums.
3 A public pawnshop.—Ed

CHAPTER IX

1 For fuller information as to Mungret the reader is referred to a paper by the Rev Denis
    Murphy, S.J., which was read at a meeting of the Royal Historical and Archaeological So-
    ciety held in Limerick, and which is published in the Journal of that Society for October,
    1889. The paper contains all the information that can be brought together in connection
    with this famous Abbey.
2 Joyce's *Irish Names of Places*, p. 318.
3 See a paper by the Rev Michael Malone in the Journal of the Royal Historical and Archaeo-
    logical Association of Ireland, 1872-73, p. 80.
4 In the Down Survey it is called Lisleane and Ballyknock and was the property of Jordan
    Roche and Edward Bourke Fitzgerald. In the reign of Charles II the lands were granted to
    the Duke of York, who, when he came to the throne, restored them to Dominick Roche,
    son of Jordan, who was created Viscount Cahiravallagh.
5 Castle Troy is called in the Down Survey Callagh Itroy or Garran Itroy and Garraneight-
    ragh. Troy is probably a phonetic reproduction of the final syllable in the Irish name.
6 Historical Memoir of the O'Briens.
7 According to the Down Survey the following lands were granted to Archbishop Boyle: –
    Carrig-o-Gunnell, 474 arable acres, Knocknalegue, Knockcunnoran, Malkino, Ballynoe,
    Cahernakilly, Tiervowe, in all 887 acres of arable and 121 of bog.

Index

P

Parteen 44
Pery, Right Hon E. S. 93
Preston, Colonel 38
Purcell, General 51

Q

Quay, George's 93
Quin, John 107

R

Rathurd 114
Rickard Tinsley, John, Mayor of Limerick 109
Rinuccini 38 - 40
Rome 25
Russell and Sons, Messrs J.N. 102
Russell, J. 103
Russell, Richard 107
Ruvigni 69, 75

S

Saingeal 18, 21, 75, 91, 114
Sarsfield, Patrick 67 - 68, 72, 76, 79, 91, 109 - 110
Scattery Island (King's Island) 18, 24, 44, 47, 71 - 72, 80, 92
Scotland 17
Scottish Highlands 67
Sexton, Edmond 84
Sgavenmore, General 71, 75, 122
Shannon, River 17, 20, 28, 42 - 44, 68 - 69, 72, 81 - 82, 88, 91 - 92, 116, 125 - 126
Shee, Sir M.A. 102
Singland 18, 21, 75, 91, 114
Sligo 42 - 43, 68
Sollohed 23
Spaight, Sir James 102
Spanish Armada 125
Spillane, William 101, 110
Spring Rice, T., Right Hon. Lord Monteagle 102, 108
St. Manchin 18
St. Munchin 80 - 82
St. Nessan 18, 112
St. Patrick 18, 91, 114, 117
St. Ruth, French officer 67 - 68, 79
St. Senan 18
Story, Dean of Limerick 122
Strafford 35
Strongbow 28 - 29
Stuart, Charles 38 - 40
Stuart, James 67 - 68, 76, 79, 81 - 82
Sulcoit 23

T

Taafe 39
Tait, Sir Peter 103, 107
Talbot, Richard, Duke of Tyrconnell 87
Talmash 75
Thomond 18
Thomond, Earl of 84, 87
Thomond, King of 26, 28 - 29, 31, 33
Thor 20
Thurles 28
Tollemache 67
Tomar 21
Treaty Stone 109
Tuthill, Colonel 44
Tyrconnell, Duke of 68, 81 - 82, 87
Tyrone, Earl of 37 - 38

U

Ulster 26
Ussher, Jocelin 114

V

Viking 22 - 23

W

Walker 104
Walker, Colonel 47
Waller, Sir Hardress 42, 47, 52
Waterford 21, 26, 28, 35, 40
Wauchop 76
Westmeath 67
Wexford 40
William of Orange 74, 77, 91 - 92, 116
Wirtemburg, Duke of 67, 77
Wirtemburg, Prince of 75
Wolfe, Father 38, 41 - 42, 50 - 51